Christopher Turner.

1864.

A NORTH WALES VILLAGE

DARTINGTON HALL
STUDIES IN RURAL SOCIOLOGY

RURAL DEPOPULATION IN ENGLAND AND
WALES, 1851–1951
by JOHN SAVILLE

THE COUNTRY CRAFTSMAN: A Study of some Rural
Crafts and the Rural Industries Organization in England
by W. M. WILLIAMS

A WEST COUNTRY VILLAGE: ASHWORTHY
Family, Kinship and Land
by W. M. WILLIAMS

THE RURAL TRANSPORT PROBLEM
by DAVID ST. JOHN THOMAS

A NORTH WALES VILLAGE
A Social Anthropological Study
by ISABEL EMMETT

A NORTH WALES VILLAGE

VILLAGE

A Social Anthropological Study

by
ISABEL EMMETT

LONDON
ROUTLEDGE & KEGAN PAUL

First published 1964
by Routledge & Kegan Paul Limited
Broadway House, 68–74, Carter Lane
London, E.C.4

Printed in Great Britain
by Cox & Wyman Limited
London, Fakenham and Reading

To my Parents
and in memory of
Griffith Griffiths

CONTENTS

Preface   *page* ix

1. Place and Values   1

2. Welsh and English   15

3. Prestige Ladders   30

4. Farming   49

5. Partisans in Peacetime   69

6. If Not That Law, Which Law?   77

7. Chapel and Church   90

8. The Role of 'Not Knowing' in the Moral
    Code   101

9. Community   119

10. Change   130

    Conclusion   142

Appendices

1. Population at each decennial census   143

2. Some information on Llan farms changing
    hands from about 1870 to 1959   144

3. Children leaving grammar school in 1937
    without taking General School Certificate
    between ages 14–16   146

    Bibliography   147

    Index   151

DIAGRAMS

Sketch Map 1   *page* xviii

Sketch Map 2   3

Borrowing   65

Shearing   67

Average age of males at marriage   109

Illegitimate births per 1,000 live
    births   109

PREFACE

THIS book is based on a study made between July 1958 and September 1962 when I lived in the parish of Llan[1] in North Wales, and in this introduction I wish to explain what I have tried to do, and attempt to answer some of the possible criticisms in advance.

I tried to observe, understand and record what people actually did, rather than what they said they did; by living among them and joining in their activities rather than by sending out questionnaires.

Man as an individual observer is a biased tool; each man, however similarly trained, sees a human situation in his own unique way and finds different aspects of it interesting. A student of society enters into social relations with the people he is studying, and the nature of those relations is determined by his outlook and by the people's attitude to him; and these relations in turn determine how he sees the society and what he sees of it.

Some current workers in the field of social anthropology think that the answer to this problem of an inevitably biased observer studying an infinitely complex subject-matter is to try to eliminate bias and individuality in the observer by telling him what questions to ask (and sometimes the voice and clothes in which to ask them); and by simplifying the subject-matter to measurable aspects which it is hoped will prove to be pointers to the complex reality. They hope that such simplification, as well as making their work more scientific, will facilitate comparisons between different societies.

But before facts can be compared we must be sure that they are facts. A team of interviewers making house-to-house calls

[1] 'Llan' is the name I have given to a parish in Merionethshire whose real name, like the names of the various parts of the parish and of individuals living in it, it seems better to disguise.

ix

around Llan would doubtless compile some interesting charts and figures which they could relate to charts and figures culled elsewhere. But the relationship between those charts and figures and life in Llan would be tenuous and the relationship between those charts and figures and the essential and distinctive features of life in a Welsh-speaking village would be, I think, non-existent.

Social anthropologists wish to make comparisons and if they did not intend to do so their work would be almost pointless. In this work in several chapters I suggest comparisons between behaviour in North Wales and in other societies. I can only suggest such comparisons with confidence when I feel I know the societies I compare, either from personal experience or because the material on them is convincing.

Attempts have been made in the past to compare isolated features of a great number of societies each of which has been studied differently and in varying degrees of thoroughness.[1] Such features, plucked out of context, are not facts, and societies of such varying size and character are not comparable, and the futility of this method has long been understood. It is not necessarily an advance to try to compare one shallow study with another; that is to compare one set of measurable 'pointers' to a society with another set, as modern aspirants to a scientific method do. For instance, it may be relatively simple to count how much a household spends on tobacco or how many kin a woman sends Christmas cards to in various communities. But these measurable pointers may not point to the same thing in each community. It is no more safe to take them as indices of a certain social set-up, assuming them to have a fixed social significance, than it is to take the amount spent by a household on tobacco as an index of the 'standard of living' in any one community. Taken in isolation from a general knowledge of the community; a knowledge of which particular sub-group the behaviour may be confined to; and what significance the behaviour has in the community in relation to the meaning of

[1] e.g. G. P. Murdock, *Social Structure* (New York 1949); and L. T. Hobhouse, G. C. Wheeler and M. Ginsberg, *The Material Culture and Social Institutions of the Simpler Peoples* (London 1915).

other kinds of behaviour; such countings and comparisons are misleading and dangerous.

The main trend discernible in current British social anthropology and that which I should like to associate myself with concentrates on the task of understanding behaviour in a particular human group, with no more ambitious aim than the hope that the results of this sufficiently taxing task may be usable for comparisons with similarly intensive studies. Information is gathered primarily in the hope that it will lead to insight, rather than for the purposes of comparison. An attempt is made to see the relevance of one kind of behaviour by trying to relate it to other kinds of behaviour in the same group. It is recognized that bias cannot be eliminated; that interpretation is happening as facts are being seen and described; that in the study of human society, at least, we are very far from separating the reporting of facts from their understanding because what we can perceive of the reality is limited by our ideas about that reality and as we continue our work the ideas we get from the facts we record again limit what further facts we can perceive.

Evans-Pritchard wrote in 1937:[1]

'Explanations . . . will be found embodied in my descriptive account and are not set forth independently of it. My interpretations are contained in the facts themselves, for I have described the facts in such a way that the interpretations emerge as part of the description.'

This seems to me to be a recognition of what inevitably happens to the student of society, and is clearer than claiming, as some writers still do, that information has been separated from interpretation. Those writers who maintain that they give enough information about the community on which they theorize for the student to judge whether or not their theories are tenable, still give only information which relates more or less directly to those theories: their interest in the theories limits their study and we have to accept their word that we have all the necessary information with which to judge the theories.

In associating myself with this main trend, I am not claiming

[1] E. E. Evans-Pritchard, *Witchcraft, Oracles and Magic among the Azande* (Oxford 1932).

for my study of Llan close kinship with the great classics of social anthropology which have given us insight into familiar ways of life.[1] Nor do I hope to evade a duty to use questionnaires, random samples and so on by putting myself in company with great names. But I think that a human society is very difficult to understand and to study, and that to ignore the difficulties is dangerous. Thinking we are scientific and behaving as though we were scientific will not make us scientific.

In her study of Bemba diet,[2] Audrey Richards showed the pitfalls which could await a nutritional expert who thought to judge food consumption in an alien culture with whose values and daily habits he was not familiar. The porridge cooked in one hut was not necessarily made for that hut's inhabitants, but might be shared among a circle of relations which was rarely the same two days running. Were certain foodstuffs sacred; others thought of as disgusting, others used as a means of currency, or for making gifts? Were food displays or herds of cattle the only outward signs of power for great men? Ignorance of the answers to such questions could invalidate conclusions based upon samples taken purely at random; correlations calculated to a nicety and all-inclusive surveys of large areas. Richards's study made it possible for administrators, economists and dietitians to appreciate such factors and to understand how and why an apparently backward, economically inefficient people behaved in the way they did.

In an unfamiliar society, intensive studies are essential and, if they rely on other methods, social anthropologists will be succumbing to those very hazards which Richards could show other experts resulted from a shallow, if 'scientific', study. North Wales was certainly to me such an unfamiliar society and was not amenable to survey methods. I tried to gain insight into it.

My English nationality was a handicap: the extent of the

[1] E. E. Evans-Pritchard's book on Azande Witchcraft for example; a book in which the author made witchcraft beliefs held by apparently superstitious savages seem comprehensible beliefs held by fellow human beings.

[2] A. I. Richards, *Land, Labour and Diet in Northern Rhodesia* (London 1939).

effect of this I was unable to gauge. This handicap was offset by the fact that I was married to a native of the parish who had lived there most of his life, and that I had children.

My methods of study were therefore limited before I began work. Having married into the community, and by doing so acquired relations and friends in the parish, I could not have 'turned official' and gone round every house with a questionnaire even had I wanted to do so. I have explained above why I do not think it proper to rely on the questionnaire approach. Certainly the most reliable results were not to be obtained in that way in Llan; many of the questions I wanted to ask could not have been answered in that way. Life in the countryside depends on people 'keeping face' even though they cannot keep secrets. Seemingly innocent questions as to dates in the family history may probe family secrets – secrets known to all the parish, but not admitted publicly, and certainly not admitted to prying outsiders.

Other questions such as the names of all members of the household, occupation and chapel affiliation could have been answered by a house-to-house call, perhaps, although even these would not necessarily have been answered fully. Many people have an inclination to mislead officials – and anyone with a form is an official – and will be reluctant to disclose facts which they cannot at the time see could be used against them – 'just in case'.

But in addition I did not wish to use the door-to-door method because taking the role of house canvasser would have clashed with my desire to participate in parish activities as much as possible.

There were other ways of answering the questions, since a few elderly people between them could answer for most households in the parish and checking could be done from records. Wherever possible I have checked and supplemented my discussion with statistical tables compiled from national sources or from local records; but I have not felt it was worth handicapping myself in my main role of social anthropologist in an effort to try playing the part of social surveyor. Where comments have been made on an area wider than Llan, evidence for making them has been a study of North Welsh newspapers over the past fifty years; periodical contact with affinal kin scattered over North Wales; periods in hospitals and travel over the area.

I have said that I tried to participate in parish activities. My participation was as a foreigner, in spite of the ready-made introduction I had to people, and all my experiences confirm the generalizations I make in this work on the attitude of Welsh-speaking people towards the English. North Welsh country people expect English people to be rich, aloof and a bit crazy; and I was suspected for some time – against all evidence – of being rich; by many held to be aloof, and by all agreed to be a bit crazy. Behaviour which would not have been condoned in a local woman, such as drinking in the pub with the men, was accepted as understandable in me. My classification thus had advantages as well as the more numerous disadvantages, and equipped with both I participated in parish activities. I was a member of the Women's Institute, a secretary of the youth club, and a tutor of a W.E.A. class in Dinas. In connection with these organizations I visited many homes in the parish. As wife of a farm-worker who helped out in different farms from week to week, I had the opportunity to visit all but two of the farms in the parish.

In this study I have not attempted to cover every aspect of social life in Llan that came to my notice. I saw apparent paradoxes and have tried to discuss them in such a way as to make the behaviour of North Welsh people comprehensible to others; so that readers might say, 'Had I been in that position I can well imagine I would have acted in the same way.' This seems to me to be one of the main tasks of social anthropology: to make meaningful to other people the apparently senseless, or mischievous or strange activity of any human group. Not because all human activity is equally useful and sensible but because before condemning, praising, trying to change or trying to conserve such behaviour we should fully understand what part it plays in the life of the group who perform it.

The paradoxes I noticed and found to be significantly related to each other were the following: Firstly that there were virtually no class distinctions in this part of Great Britain, though trains, radio, visitors, films and television make North Wales a part of that larger society which is very conscious of class and status differences. Secondly, that people in North Wales caught a lot of salmon at the time of the year when such fishing was poaching but did not do so to satisfy an economic demand. They did not eat them all, they did not sell them and sometimes they did not find it easy to dispose of them. Thirdly, that a high rate of illegitimacy existed in a district where the influence of the chapel on people's lives is relatively very strong and where the chapels frown severely on illegitimacy. This book is an attempt to answer the questions raised in my mind by those paradoxes.

To give a background to the discussion of these subjects, in the first two chapters I describe briefly the parish and some of the values of its people; and the attitude that its Welsh inhabitants have towards English people. In the third chapter I discuss the lack of class distinctions between the Welsh people of the parish. In the fourth chapter I describe farming in Llan and discuss the basis on which farmers co-operate. In the fifth chapter I discuss poaching and in the sixth anti-officialdom generally and local alternatives to British bureaucracy. In the seventh chapter I treat the role of the chapel in parish life and in the preservation of Welsh culture and this chapter serves as an introduction to the discussion in the eighth chapter of how Llan people reconcile their adherence to Methodism with their actual behaviour. In the ninth chapter I have tried to see whether the theories which Ronald Frankenberg put forward as a result of his study of a Welsh village had any relevance to Llan, and the final chapter deals with social change.

There is no chapter specifically on kinship although such a chapter usually can be found in works of social anthropology written today. In my four years in Llan I made extensive inquiries into kinship links within the parish, kinship links beyond the parish, co-operation and contact between near and distant kin, the recognition of and behaviour towards distant kin, marriage relationships and child up-bringing. County archives, parish registers, old school and court registers, gravestones, old people's memories, were searched to provide genealogies. But I do not write specifically about family life and kinship links because my inquiries into this subject did not reveal anything of significance about kinship and family life in themselves, or anything that would throw light on the other problems I wanted to discuss. Llan people rely on their kin in times of need; very few Llan families are without kin in the parish; funerals in North Wales are important gatherings of kin as well as measures of status. These points could be stretched to fill a monograph. I have mentioned kinship only when it seemed relevant to what I wanted to say. Facts purveyed in themselves and by themselves are not only dull; they are not true in any important sense unless they are related to each other in a general analysis of the social situation. They have little meaning unless they are understood and fitted into a pattern. There are many possible patterns into which to fit them and many possible truths, but isolated facts, of the kind collected by the team of technique-laden surveyors I have postulated in my cartoon of the scientific social anthropologist above, are not sociological facts. It is not just that such interviewers are told lies or do not see the whole truth. They do not see or collect or write down sociological facts about human groups if they see them as unrelated.

I have said above that in this book I have tried to explain paradoxical behaviour so that others will understand it and the part that it plays in the life of North Wales. In my explanations, I have not always related the behaviour to motives in the actors' minds, and Llan people finding their actions discussed in this book would perhaps protest that they would not be more snobbish to each other if English people were never seen in the parish: that they were just not snobbish people; or that they did not feel when they went poaching that they did so to beat the officials or to get closer to each other and if they did not feel these were the reasons why they acted in the way they did, how could they be the reasons? My answer is that when a sociologist gives an explanation of behaviour in terms of its final effect on the group performing it, he stands to be proven wrong if they cease to perform that behaviour and the group does not change in the way he implied it would without that behaviour; or if the group changes in ways that should but do not affect that behaviour, according to his theory. But he should not be tested by what people believe makes them act. He should not feel obliged, since he is not competent, to reduce his explanations to psychological terms and if he cannot find conscious motives which fit he should not feel he ought to invent unconscious ones. To do so would be dishonest.

The social forces that give some London boroughs high suicide rates, and others high juvenile delinquency rates, break up into countless particular pressures acting separately and in different combinations on the mind of each individual suicide or delinquent. The sociologist's correlation of social isolation with suicide or poverty with juvenile delinquency and his thesis which uses the correlation as part of an explanation, do not depend on his ability to turn psychologist and translate the correlation into individual motivations.

I have taken as my unit the parish of Llan, and have taken the Electoral Register as a basis to work on. There is, however, a section at the lower or southern part of the parish, which whilst it belongs administratively to the parish of Llan, for shopping, religious, educational and social activities belongs to the neighbouring parish and I have not included this part of the parish in my study. When I say 'the parish of Llan' I mean in fact the parish of Llan except for the part cut off by the thick black line in Sketch Map 1. Thus while the parish of Llan had a population of 532 (over three years of age) at the last census in 1951, my population in 1959 numbered 346 of whom 329 were over three. Most of the families I exclude vote in the neighbouring parish and there is a separate electoral register for them.

Unless otherwise stated, figures and other data refer to 1959.

I could have taken as my unit one of the villages in the parish; I did not do so partly because each village was too small to contain representatives of all the groups I wished to mention and partly because a division of function exists between the various parts of the parish. The hamlet of Aber, which in 1960 had only four Welsh families left in it, points to a future for rural North Wales which many Nationalists fear. The village of Dinas houses white-collared workers and some English people as well as manual workers, and, as the centre of the parish, is the main scene of its conflicts and festivities. The hamlet of Pensarn, housing Welsh-speaking manual workers only, is an untidy version of the undifferentiated community Llan people would like their whole community to be. The village of Carmel houses the chapel-going sheep-farmers with memories of the

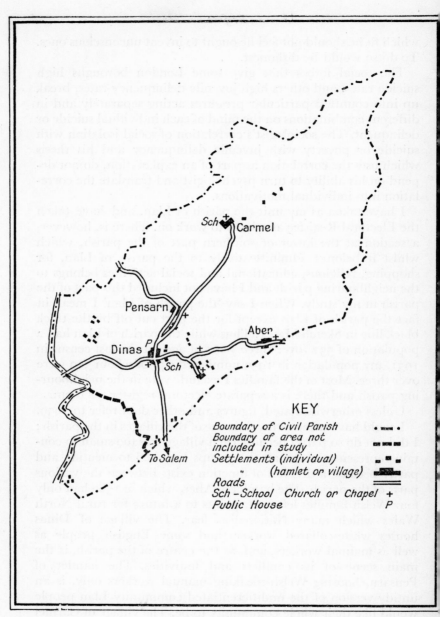

SKETCH MAP I.

old ways: it stands for the conscience and the tradition of the parish.

Five people in the parish are English people who have married local inhabitants. I have not spoken about them because, although they are regarded as outsiders, they are assimilated to a fair degree and to the extent that they are not, they are isolated from each other as much as from the Welsh community. They do not act together, as the visiting English intellectuals do, and so they are not sociologically a group.

I studied social anthropology at the London School of Economics from 1954 to 1958 and have to thank the staff of the social anthropology department there for all I know on the subject. The first two years of my study of Llan were very part-time, since I had no financial help except my husband's. In the last six months, through the kind intervention of the staff of the Institute of Community Studies, I received a grant from the Dartington Hall Trust which enabled me to complete the work and I am very grateful for this help.

In and around Llan, many people helped me and in particular I wish to thank Mrs. E. Ellis, Mrs. A. Evans, Mrs. M. Evans, Mr. E. W. Jones, the Rev. E. Jones, Mr. and Mrs. R. Owen, Mr. and Mrs. D. C. Williams and Mr. R. A. Williams for their help, information and patient criticism, and Mr. Tom Kinsey for the loan of his books. I also wish to thank Professor J. Barnes, Mr. E. Cooper-Willis, Mr. A. D. Rees, Mrs. Susan Serafy, Mr. W. M. Williams and Dr. Michael Young for advice and criticism. I had two professional co-workers to whom my debt is obviously great: Mr. John Hilton did the maps and Mr. Robin Emmett prepared the statistical tables. Only my husband knows how much this book owes to him.

The bibliography consists of works to which I have referred and works from which I have quoted. In cases where I have quoted, the publishers' names are included in the bibliography and I should like to thank them for their permission to make such quotations. Except in the instance in which the publisher's name is given, I have to thank H.M.S.O. for permission to quote from Government publications. Lord Raglan kindly allowed me to quote from his article in *Wales*.

CHAPTER ONE

PLACE AND VALUES

THE part of Great Britain I wish to describe is the parish of Llan in Welsh-speaking North Wales. As far as the inhabitants of Llan are concerned, the parts of Wales where English is spoken are not Wales at all.[1] Indeed, they sometimes speak as though North Wales were the only true Wales, although the western counties of Carmarthenshire and Cardiganshire are as Welsh-speaking as any of their home counties of Anglesey, Caernarvonshire and Merionethshire. For brevity's sake I shall refer to North Wales when I mean Welsh-speaking North Wales. This includes Merionethshire, Caernarvonshire (except for the seaside resorts), Anglesey (these three north-western counties together making up the administrative district of Gwynedd, and the heart of North Wales), part of North Montgomeryshire and parts of Denbighshire. Much of what applies to Llan can be extended fairly confidently to the rest of Welsh-speaking North Wales; most of it to Gwynedd. I cannot speak of the western counties of Carmarthen and Cardigan. Where Llan is untypical, I shall try to make it clear.

The parish of Llan is very beautiful. It lies in mountainous country, its mountain slopes rising sharply from a very flat valley. The sea is not far from its borders, so that from its mountain farms the sea and the estuary of the main river, the Stwlan, can be seen very clearly. The soil is very poor, with few exceptions the only crop grown is hay, the mountains are snow-covered for much of the winter, the flat land is peaty and very

---

[1] In *A History of Modern Wales*, London 1950; David Williams writes 'The division of Wales into two nations, the one rural in its occupation and Welsh in speech, the other English and industrial, two nations between whom there were few cultural ties, was the work of the nineteenth century.'

wet for most of the year and is criss-crossed with ditches. In this environment, living has always been hard and the traditional pattern of settlement is one of scattered houses and hamlets rather than compact villages. The parish contains two hamlets – Pensarn and Aber and many scattered farmsteads, as well as the two small villages of Carmel and Dinas. Sketch Map 2 shows the physical geography of the parish.

Merioneth has been losing its population[1] in the last 80 years. Slate quarries have been closing down largely as a result of competition from the tile industry; the small ports which grew up around the business of shipping slates have lost their trade. Furthermore, every decade, larger farms are needed to provide a living and the smallholdings have been and are being amalgamated and the deserted stone farm-houses, minute by English standards, are taken as holiday houses by English people.

Although all the empty houses and holiday houses in the parish are isolated farmsteads, in addition to these, scattered dwellings house about half the population of the parish and in the past the proportion not living in the hamlets and villages was clearly much greater than it is now. Sketch Map 1 shows the lay-out of the parish. I call Dinas and Carmel villages on the arbitrary grounds that their schools are still functioning. Dinas is the social centre of the parish. It consists of a public house – the only one in the parish; two shops, one of which is a post office as well as a general store; two churches – the old, which is very rarely used, and the new, which is attended by a visiting minister; a Methodist chapel; and houses for a population of 107.

Aber had its own school until 1944. Now that its population has shrunk to fourteen, the school has been closed and the three children of primary school age are taken the two miles to Dinas school in a car. The Methodist chapel at Aber has had no

---

[1] In 1884 the intake into Dinas school was 31; in 1949, it was 4. Between 1931 and 1951 in the rural areas of North-West Wales there was a decrease of 4,000 in the population, if gains where service camps were located are not counted. S. Jones and G. P. Smith, *Employment and Unemployment in N. W. Wales* (Bangor 1960). Their survey area covered Angelsey, Caernarvon, most of Merioneth and parts of Denbigh and Flint. For further details, see Appendix 1.

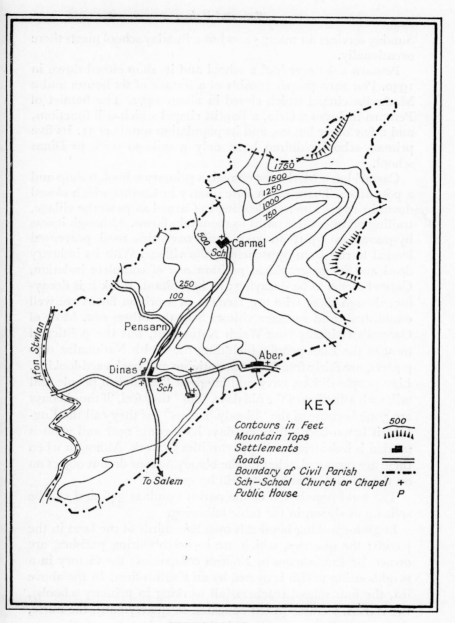

Contours in Feet
Mountain Tops
Settlements
Roads
Boundary of Civil Parish
Sch—School Church or Chapel +
Public House P

1750
1500
1250
1000
750
500
Carmel
Sch
250
100
Pensarn
Aber
P
Dinas
Sch
Afon Stwlan
To Salem

KEY

500

Sunday services for many years but a Sunday school meets there occasionally.

Pensarn has never had a school and its shop closed down in 1930. Pen Sarn proper consists of a terrace of six houses and a Methodist chapel which closed in about 1952. The hamlet of Pensarn includes a farm, a Baptist chapel which still functions, and a few other houses, and its population numbers 31. Its five primary-school children have only a mile to walk to Dinas school.

Carmel has a Methodist chapel, a primary school, a shop and a post office. There was a slate quarry in Carmel which closed down in 1930. The road leading to Carmel stops at the village, trailing off into a few paths to mountain farms. Although it was by-passed in 1961, an arch built over this road prevented loaded lorries from approaching the village. With its industry dead and its geographical position one of complete isolation, Carmel seems to be decaying: its inhabitants think it is decaying, though those who are farmers or work on farms are well established, and summer visitors help the others out. Most of Carmel's residents vote Welsh Nationalist, but the politics of most of the Llan people, including the Welsh Nationalist supporters, are fairly free from romanticism and backward-looking. Llan people dislike, envy and laugh at the English people and talk with affection of the old days. 'But,' they feel, 'if the old days are gone because of the "bloody Saxons" [as they call the English] it is too bad – the new days have come now and what is needed is industries and opportunities to work. Although when these are proposed, what do the bloody Saxons do but object on on the grounds that beauty will be spoilt!'

The total population of the parish numbers 346 and can be split up as shown in the table following.

English-speaking landlords own two-thirds of the land in the parish; the quarries, which are in neighbouring parishes, are owned by Englishmen or English companies; the factory in a neighbouring parish is owned by an English firm. In the above list, the four school teachers (all working in primary schools), the W.E.A. lecturer (a self-educated ex-quarryman), the nurse, the apprentice surveyor and the agricultural executive are

Working Population of Llan Divided by Occupation

Total population		*Working Population – Welsh and English*	
Men	109	Farmers and workers	41	Clerks	8
		on farms		Shopkeepers and	
Women	132	Factory	15	assistants	8
		Domestic workers	13	School teachers	4
Children	105	Miscellaneous manual		Salesmen	2
——		workers	14	Insurance agent	1
		Quarry	11	W.E.A. lecturer	1
Total	346	Roads – cleaning		Agricultural Exec.	1
——		and mending	7	Nurse	1
		Builders	2	Surveyor's apprentice	1
			——	Authors	2
				Engineer	1
		Total of manual		Publisher	1
		workers	103	Designer	1
			——	Economic adviser	1
				Manufacturer	1
					——
				Total of non-manual	
				workers	34
					——

Total : 137

Welsh, but the last six 'class 1'[1] occupations on the list are followed only by English residents. This is the first illustration of one of the main themes of this work, which is to show in detail the lack of class divisions among the Welsh-speaking inhabitants of North Wales and the way in which the English take the place of the upper, upper-middle or ruling class, nationalism being the way through which class antagonisms are expressed.

Another interesting feature of social stratification in Llan is the fact that farmers do not form a separate status group, and the reasons for this are discussed in Chapter Four. Most Llan

[1] i.e. included in the Registrar General's classification of Class 1 occupations.

farmers do not own their own farms; farming was for long a poorly paying trade and until recently it has been classed among the various manual jobs a man could do. Another reason will serve to introduce the picture of their own parish which Llan people have. It is said of farming in other parts of Great Britain : 'It is not a job so much as a way of life.' By this is meant that farmers make little division between working and living. But for the bulk of the Llan population, farmers and non-farmers, 'living' and 'working' are not separate. The people that a man works with are often the people he sees in the evening. If they do not live in the parish, they will nevertheless be known by the people in the parish, so that news about them is interesting to a man's family and to his friends. The quarries are fourteen miles away but one Llan man under 30 whom I asked estimated that he knew a third of the population of the quarry town by sight and he was not untypical. The factory is outside the parish and three miles away, but most Llan people know everyone in the factory village by sight. Whether he works in the quarry or in the factory or cleans the roads or works on a farm, a man will see his friends and relatives during the day, will learn gossip worth recounting and recall times and people well known to all. A Llan man forgoes a holiday not for the reason he gives, i.e. that he cannot afford it, but above all because he does not want to go on holiday. He does not have the feeling that he wants to get away from it all: his life forms a satisfactory whole. He is interested in his community. When I asked people questions about how this man was related to that, or who lived in X farm before Evans had moved into it, a discussion on the matter began which could well have taken place without my having started it. Llan people enjoy talking about their parish and its population; in doing so they refresh and bring up to date their mental picture of the community. I have explained that this mental picture has a radius spreading far beyond the parish in space. Depending on where they have worked, where their relations live, or where they themselves have lived, outside the parish, different individuals will know different areas, but if one could superimpose one on top of the other the mental pictures which each Llan person has of the district, the overall picture would be one with Llan clearly delineated in the centre, the clarity of the rest of the picture diminishing as neighbouring parishes recede in distance.

In space a Llan man's mental picture of his community is an area of hills and valleys, the central part of which he knows by every bump, ditch and stone and which he can run over in the dark safely if necessary, populated by individuals and families that he knows from very well to slightly. But his mental picture also has depth in time. It is not like a snapshot taken of Llan and neighbouring district on 10th October, 1959. Each person carries his past round with him. A courting couple who stop going out together still have to see each other and will continue to meet when they are married to other people and have families and grow old. In a city a man often moves on in space as he moves on in time. In Llan, people are related to places according to their histories and this is best shown by the way in which people are referred to.

A simple example is that of Mr. William Evans who lives in a house and on a smallholding called Galon uchaf and who is invariably referred to as Will Galon uchaf. He has lived at Galon uchaf most of his life. Other cases are not so simple. There are three complicating factors of naming-by-place to be taken into account.

Firstly, people will be known by the name of a certain farm or house whilst they live or even only work in that place, but may, afterwards, be called by the name of another place, by most people. Thus Harold Williams was called Harry Parcglas when he lived at Parcglas; he was called Harry Penylan when he lived at Penylan, but when he left Penylan to move to Hafod, he remained at Hafod until his death and was referred to, and still is referred to, by most people as Harry Williams Hafod.

Secondly, some people are referred to in different ways by different people. John Jones's first home was a farm called Pwll-du. He later lived on a smallholding called Wern, and for the last eight years he has lived in the Council houses. A man of 28 who remembers him chiefly from the time when he was at Wern refers to him as John the Wern. A man of 50, who remembers him chiefly from the time when he was at Pwll-du, refers to him as John Pwll-du.

Thus to a certain extent the time depth of a man's mental picture of his community can be told by the way he refers to others.

The third factor to be taken into account is that special circumstances, apart from the age of the speaker, may influence the name by which a man is known. One of the places in which he lived may have seemed appropriate to his character. Edward Jones Pont Ddu has lived in the Council houses for eight years but he is not the type one associates with the modern, well-equipped Council houses. He is an elderly working man, who likes his beer; most of the stories told about him refer to the time when he lived in Pont Ddu; he is the sort to live in an old cottage in the mountains like Pont Ddu and so he will continue to be called Edward Jones Pont Ddu. Harriet and Peter Dennis, on the other hand, are not strongly associated with any other place in people's minds and are called Harriet and Peter Tai Council, although they have lived in the Council houses for only two years. Edward Lewis lived for two years at Y Gesail, for seven years at Ty Isaf and after that lived at Bryn for a year before finally moving out of the parish. He still visits the parish and he and his family are spoken of. He is referred to as Ned Y Gesail. It was in his first years in the parish, when he was at Y Gesail, that he made an impression on the parish and he will always be known to Llan people as Ned Y Gesail. His children, who are remembered toiling up and down the mountainside from Ty Isaf to school and back are known as the Ty Isaf children.

'Now[1] Ty Isaf' is the name given in Llan to Owen Williams, a dealer in cattle and sheep of some considerable wealth, who now lives on a farm eighteen miles away. It is thirty years since he lived in Ty Isaf, though he has farmed other places in Llan since then. One of the reasons why he is always referred to as 'Now Ty Isaf' is that this name puts him on a level socially with Llan people; it makes him sound like a neighbour, a very ordinary fellow; it relates the speaker in some way to a rich man and reminds everyone of the early ordinary days of Now Ty Isaf.

Some people, then, like Ned Y Gesail and Now Ty Isaf, are

[1] 'Now' is a local abbreviation of Owen.

referred to in the same way by most people because for everyone
that name suits them best, or places them in the way people
want them placed. Some people, like Will Galon uchaf, are
referred to in the same way by most people because they have
lived all or most of their lives in one place.

But as I mentioned as the first complicating factor, some
people are referred to in different ways by different groups.
Since, in the case of John Jones, mentioned above, a man of 50
will have known him, not only when he was at Pwll-du, but also
after that, when he was at Wern, why does the man of 50 not
call him the Wern as does the man of 28? Jones was much
longer at Wern, but to the 50-year-old man, Jones's years at
Pwll-du are the ones in which he knew him best, lived nearest
to him, or formed his picture of him.

Although most people are referred to by different names at
different times in their lives and many people are referred to by
different names according to the generation and perhaps preference of the speaker, there is no confusion. Llan people know
the histories of their neighbours and even though young people
do not remember their elders living in this or that place, they
know that they did live there.

Of the 241 adults in Llan, 77 have the surname Jones or the
surname Williams. The names Evans, Griffiths, Roberts and
Owen account for another 54. There is no great variety of
Christian names to help either. Certain naming practices
appear to be devices to avoid the apparent confusion resulting
from the few surnames. Thus one John Jones is called John
Laura Wyn, his mother having the Christian names Laura Wyn.
Another John Jones is called John Bunbury, his wife's maiden
name being Bunbury. His brother is called Jim Bunbury since
he too is connected with this usefully distinctive name. But it
will be seen from the above that other naming practices add to
the confusion – a confusion which exists only for outsiders.
What all the naming practices do is to express relationships
between young and old, age-mate and age-mate, near and far
neighbour, and between people and places.

Age differences are also expressed by terms of address. A
man will say to a man or woman of the same age or younger
than himself:

9

'How art thou, John?'

'How art thou, Kate?'

To a man older than himself he will say:

'How are you, John Hughes?'

To a woman older than himself he will say:

'How are you, Mrs. Hughes?'

He will be speaking Welsh, and to people he knows, when he uses these greetings. He will use the formal 'you', rather than 'thou' to a man older than himself, even if the man is his work-mate whom he sees every day.

Some of the elderly white-collared workers, such as the head-master of Dinas school, the minister and the postmaster, are addressed sometimes by those younger than themselves as 'Mister', but that is a word rarely used between Welsh people of Llan to or about Welsh people of Llan, and I have heard a man say about Anglesey, 'They use a lot of style up there – they call each other "Mister."' In conversation about them, these elderly white-collared workers are referred to by young and old as John Tai Coch, Gwyn Post, Wmffra School and so on, in the same way as others are referred to. This slight and infrequent distinction in address is a correct indication of the slightness of status differences in the parish.

Llan people see the people of their community in terms of places and see farms and cottages with families attached, and both people and places are always seen embedded in and em-broidered by the history of Llan's past fifty-odd years. This history is not one of important events: the two world wars left the lives of most Llan people unmarked. It is a history of scandal and jokes, a gossip history, whose power on people and beauty for people it is hard to express. Part of the power derives from the fact that everyone is familiar with that past; anyone can describe it.

People walked everywhere, slept too many people to a room, on lumpy mattresses, and carried icy water from a stream; the men battled with recalcitrant animals, the women with mud. In May and November, if they had disagreed with their masters they went to the fairs to be hired. The farmers walked up and down looking the workers over and finally offered a man or girl so much for half a year 'if they went to chapel on Sundays', and gave them a penny to seal the bargain. Others went to the fairs to fight, flirt and watch.

They sat through interminable sermons in chapel, walked miles to choir practice and sang with pleasure. Some of the quarrymen lived all week in the barracks up in the heart of the mountain and only came down to their wives at week-ends. They walked up with their fellow quarrymen, lived with them, worked with them, walked down with them and went to Sunday school and chapel with them. They worked in the hay with them in the summer evenings and Saturday afternoons when work in the quarry was over.

Much of the life was like country life anywhere. But the chapel was woven through it all in a way that gave it distinction. Moreover, that which makes country life meaningful is the talk; and the talk was in Welsh and so the whole life was peculiarly Welsh. The very bleakness of the life made the talk rich and Llan people learnt everything from that talk. They learnt the unique culture in which they lived. Quarrymen talked philosophy; relatives talked kinship; farmers talked economics; everybody talked religion and scandal. So people learnt to think of their community past and present, in the light of their system of values, which are not only 'country' values, but also emphatically 'Welsh' values. The whole of that past life was strongly imbued with the essence of Welshness which is so attractive that its much fainter presence pulls the English intellectuals back to Llan year after year and makes them wish to settle there.

In his study of a Welsh-speaking village in Cardiganshire[1] David Jenkins described two distinct and separate ways of life, buchedd A and buchedd B (the Welsh word 'buchedd' meaning 'way of life'); the first that of the 'religious people' and the second that of the 'tavern people'. Buchedd A people are the leaders in chapel; they are thrifty; they respect education and knowledge; they try to get their children to get on in the world regardless of whether or not it involves them leaving Wales. Buchedd B people ride motor-cycles, stand on street corners; drink; relax on Sundays. People who follow one way of life do

[1] D. Jenkins and others, *Welsh Rural Communities*, Ed. E. Davies and A. D. Rees (Cardiff 1960).

not marry people who follow the other. In their introduction
to the book, Mr. Elwyn Davies and Mr. Alwyn Rees express the
opinion that such a division is general in Wales.

In Llan buchedd A and buchedd B are not separate. At a
superficial glance the division appears to be there. There are
certainly some people, and a large proportion of Carmel's
population, who take an active part in chapel affairs, never
drink, are thrifty and hard-working. But unlike Jenkins's
buchedd A people, most of them value Wales more than they
value worldly achievement: they would rather see their sons
shovelling manure or working in the factory than see them go to
London. They would like their children as individuals to have
good jobs and good opportunities, but they know that to get
them they would have to leave the community. Some, of course,
cannot afford to send their children farther on; some of the
farmers think that learning to farm the well-equipped holdings
of these post-war days is opportunity enough. But if these
farmers were from Kent or Lincoln they would probably send
their sons to agricultural college and give their daughters some
kind of higher education. For these, and for others who could
send their children 'farther on', the community wins. The fact
that intelligent, well-informed people have stayed in the community in the past means that the community is worth staying
in now. The people of Llan are individuals, as memorable as
characters in a Dickens novel. This is how the 'almost buchedd
A' people see their fellows: not, in the main, as an opposing
group, but as individuals: some exasperating, some wonderful
and this is how they themselves are seen. Their children are,
therefore, not kept apart: that would be a strange idea in Llan;
their children intermarry with people who drink, mix with
drinkers and probably drink themselves.

The Welsh value system is a relatively coherent mixture of
chapel and all which the chapel is against, but which is Welsh.
Those who go regularly to chapel and those who do not, tell the
same stories, admire the same characters and do not feel part of
the 'respectable' or 'disreputable' group so much as they feel
part of the Welsh-speaking community of North Wales.

The frequent presence of English visitors and the constant
presence of the anglicized landlords and English people with

top jobs, make Llan people very aware of their Welshness, and what permits the presence of apparently contradictory elements in their value system is the fact that all elements in it are Welsh. In the presence of the enemy, Welshness is the primary value; deacon and drunkard are friends, old schisms become unimportant.

Being religious is Welsh and in varying degrees Llan people are religious. Just as Welsh as religion is good singing, eloquence, skill in writing and reciting poetry, country craftsmanship, physical endurance, sex permissiveness before marriage, cunning and hypocrisy, and all these are part of the Welsh value system. The heroes of a Llan child are not those who went to a University and made their way in the world, but men who cut the hay in David's field in one morning with a scythe; built that high curved dry-stone wall by the mill; carried 150 lb. up the mountainside to Gelli without a pause; won so many Eisteddfod chairs; could sing 'Yr eneth ga'dd ei gwrthod' so movingly that 'the song was banned in the pubs to stop people committing suicide'. New heroes, 'pop' singers and film stars, are appearing, but they have not ousted the Welsh heroes yet. Young men, who in England would be wearing smart suits and working in offices, come from the tractor to the pub to hear and retell with glee tales of the 'real individuals' of the old days. Morgan Williams is still courting the girls at 74 – and still getting them. Cunning Will Felin, in court as a bankrupt farmer, answered every question with the words: 'I'm completely illiterate.' Another farmer, asked recently in court whether he wished to give evidence in Welsh replied: 'I don't know why you bother with that English round here.' Hedd Wyn was a shepherd killed in the 1914–18 war who won the Chair in 1917 at the National Eisteddfod, for his poetry, but was dead in France when the Eisteddfod was held, and that year is called the year of the Black Chair. Englyn (alliterative verses of old Welsh style) are sung in his memory in every pub from Caernarvon to Aberystwyth now. The ambition to write a good englyn lurks in every Llan heart and the desire to sing well, in tune and the correct voice, is very often realized. Mrs. Jones, who supports her family by going out to work as a cleaner, intends to collect and publish her father's poems. She, her teenage daughter who is learning to type, and her sister who keeps a boarding-house, travelled seventy miles to a library to look through old papers in which the poems had appeared and this expedition cause no comment or surprise in the parish. The time has not yet come when a farmhand is ashamed of singing in a choir or writing poetry, and pride in work is felt and commonly expressed, a man not only feeling good and being admired when he has thatched a haystack, made a scythe really sharp, or built a wall with no cement, but also when he has taken a tractor to pieces and put it together again successfully.

I have tried in the preceding paragraphs to describe what I mean by 'Welshness', a word I shall use often in this work. The disparate but 'Welsh' elements in the value system are held together by those concerned pretending, when they are in certain 'publics', not to know about the 'frowned-on' behaviour.

CHAPTER TWO

WELSH AND ENGLISH

IN order to understand the picture a Llan man has of 'the Saxons', it is necessary to look at the picture he has of himself, and in particular the view he has of his economic position.

One of the difficulties here is that the Llan man shows two contradictory pictures of himself and thus makes it hard to grasp how he really sees himself.

First, for sound economic reasons, he wishes to appear, as an individual, richer than he is. As I explain in Chapter Four on farming methods, economic life in Llan depends to a large extent on exchanges of goods and services in which money plays no part. Sometimes a long time elapses before one particular service is reciprocated. Confidence between partners is essential, especially as bluff plays an important part in the conduct of all negotiations and people have more confidence in a rich than a poor man.

A Canadian writer[1] recounts the maddening conversation he had when trying to buy a farm in North Wales. He knew the owner wanted to sell; the seller was so diffident and non-communicative that at one stage the author got the impression that the farm must belong to someone quite different.

In the pub, a man who wants to buy a calf talks to a man with a calf to sell.

'What price are calves making now, Huw?'

'Why? Do you want one?'

'Oh, no. No . . .' and the speaker goes off to play a game of darts.

Rees writes:[2]

'Except in cases of emergency, a farmer will not go to

[1] T. Firbank, *I Bought a Mountain* (London 1940).
[2] A. D. Rees, *Life in a Welsh Countryside* (Cardiff 1950).

another's house in a "business-like" manner to request or offer a favour. He will call as though he were only paying a friendly visit, converse with his neighbour for an hour or two, and, perhaps, partake of a meal with the family. Then when he is on the point of leaving he will mention his mission as though it were an afterthought: "Oh yes, I was wondering whether you could . . ." . . . But strange as it may seem to the outsider, the custom is not just humbug, it is a form of politeness. A favour can only be justified by friendliness, and friendliness means that one finds pleasure in the other's company and does not grudge spending time with him.'

Although Rees describes the motive as politeness, and the factors he mentions are certainly present, in my experience this indirect approach, which is just one example of the tortuous 'gamesmanship' approach found in all social relations in North Wales, is motivated more by a wish to gain an advantage than by a wish to please. When a man has spent the evening chatting and he 'casually' asks his host, or guest, just before parting, to do something for him, he wants to make it appear that he does not want the favour really; it is nothing to him. He wishes to minimize the value of the service he is asking and give the impression that he does not need help from anyone; that he is not poor.

This approach is used by labourers taking on jobs. They are sure that they will get a better rate if they make it clear that they do not need the job; 'may be able to fit it in some time'; 'don't mind doing it for Wern'. This may result in wages being owed to them for some time but they prefer not to ask for the money. The local shops will bridge the gap, but here again the borrower says he has no cash on him, and pretends that it is not poverty but just being carefree about money that results in his having his goods 'put down'.

Just as it is economically advantageous, so it is socially advantageous for a man to appear richer than he is. He wishes to convey that he has made smart deals, selling or buying at the right time. He covets a reputation as a good farmer or a good worker. Thus it is not considered polite to appear to know that so many sheep or cows died at X farm this winter. To mention it might be to imply criticism of the farmer. Money receives respect. I met a little girl of 8 who believed that one had to pay to get to heaven.[1]

Each man, then, wishes himself to be seen as well off by comparison with his neighbours. On the other hand, the Llan man thinks of himself as one of the poor Welsh country people. I wrote in Chapter One that Llan was situated in a poor part of Wales. This is true. Everyone over 40 can remember many households where bread and buttermilk made the midday meal every day and there are many people in the parish who were brought up on that kind of diet, when money was scarce and butter was bartered in the shop for tea and sugar. Some took their lunch to school in a can: buttermilk and oatcakes; the lid of the can serving as a plate. This is implicit in many details of the way they live. It might be suggested that the figures given below of *per capita* spending in the shops would be false in these circumstances, because people in Merioneth would not spend their money in shops. But I do not think there is now very much 'putting money by in a stocking'. It can be seen that people think they are poor not so much from the fact that they do not spend their money as from the way they spend it.

A farmer who lives three miles from the nearest shop does not buy a car, though everyone knows he could and that it would save him pounds in time. Another farmer has not connected electricity to his farm and spends hours chopping wood, looking after paraffin lamps and cooking on a smoky fire. These are the same men who will be very uninterested, if someone wants to buy something they have. When acting as dealers, they pretend to be rich; at home on the farm they act as though they were poor.

The diet of Llan people shows their idea of their own poverty. Boiled potatoes, fried eggs and bread and butter appear in terrible monotony on the tables. Before the war, a diet of milk products, eggs, bread, potatoes, and bacon was common. Spices, sweet things, meat, apart from home-cured bacon, and fresh fruit, were rare luxuries and the farm-worker who does not take sugar in his tea is to this day considered a good man. What

---

[1] The same attitude is not found in all small farming communities. See Pitt-Rivers's study of a Spanish village, *The People of the Sierra* (London 1954).

farm-house cooking tradition there was embraced mainly milk products, types of bread and jam, since when fruit was available it was preserved. Travellers, from Giraldus Cambrensis in the twelfth century onwards, have commented on the food. 'The kitchen does not supply many dishes, nor high-seasoned incitements to eating,' wrote Giraldus Cambrensis.[1]

'Milk and buttermilk, either alone or with potatoes, are regarded as a favourite food . . .' writes Edmund Hyde Hall.[2]

'No butcher's meat, no wheaten bread, no wine, no spirits; oat and barley bread, ale, porter and eggs commonly make the improvident stranger's repast,' wrote Nicholas Owen in 1792, describing accommodation in a North Welsh alehouse.[3]

The often-told story of Beti Jones's supper describes how Beti Jones's twenty-five children each wanted something different for supper. The joke of the story is that, with her patience exhausted, one day she mixed all the things together in one big bowl. But what makes the story of interest is that each of the twenty-five suppers asked for was a different mixture of some kind of flour or bread with water or some kind of milk product – whey, buttermilk or milk, with the exception of one supper, which was 'potatoes in buttermilk'.

In other household affairs the old families were generally from necessity keen economists – they looked for good cloth and went every twenty years to the same tailor who had supplied their family with good cloth before.

After the war, there was more money about, the shops were full of tinned foods, shop bread and biscuits were brought to the door, shop jam could be bought, milk could be sold for a good price, and so, inevitably, the old diet went. The tradition of cooking which existed involved the use of so few foods and ones so different from those now available, that it did not help the young housewife in making use of her new plenty. The tinned foods that appeared in the shops were not regarded as the

[1] Giraldus Cambrensis, *Itinerary Through Wales*, Ed. W. Ll. Williams (London 1935).

[2] E. Hyde Hall, *A Description of Carnarvonshire 1809–1811*, Ed. E. Gwynne-Jones, Caernarvonshire Historical Society Record, Series No. 2 (Caernarvon 1952).

[3] N. Owen, *Caernarvonshire, a Sketch of its History, Antiquity, Mountains and Productions* (London 1792).

materials for a new and more varied diet, but as luxuries to be brought out for visitors and special occasions. The materials of the old diet were no longer available, fewer vegetables were grown as farming changed from subsistence farming to farming for the market. People continued to eat a lot of bread, bought instead of home-made, did not eat a great deal more meat than before, ate plenty of eggs, and boiled potatoes, and had 'pudding' or desert more often. The making of stews and casseroles, different ways of cooking potatoes, the use of the variety of vegetables and fruits that can be bought in the shops did not become common.[1] Richard Hoggart's description of working-class diet in towns in Northern England between the wars sounds exotic by comparison. He writes: 'Something tasty is the key-phase in feeding. . . . There is a great range of favourite savouries, often by-products – black-puddings, pig's feet, liver, cowheel, tripe, polony, "ducks" chitterlings (and for special occasions pork-pies, which are extremely popular); and the fishmongers' savouries – shrimps, roe, kippers and mussels.'[2] The beef-dripping for breakfast and celery and radishes for tea, which every working-class Londoner knows, never appear on Llan tables. The diet is poor and monotonous and is relieved only by 'tins for visitors'.

Llan people are as unwilling to part with cash as their parents were on most traditional items, such as food, rent and furniture. But they do not save the extra money they now earn so much as spend it in a way that suggests they do not realize fully that they have it.

Spending patterns in working-class districts of Great Britain generally have been disrupted by the post-war prosperity. But it is easier for housewives in towns to translate that prosperity into a rise in the level of all parts of their life: food, housing, furniture, holidays, clothing, entertainments. They have shops, neighbours and advertisements all around them showing how

---

[1] This was written in 1959. In 1960 frozen food came to Dinas and could be the means of introducing more variety. Lack of good shopping facilities clearly contributes to the monotony of the diet. Fish, for instance, comes to the neighbouring town from the other side of England. Fruit and to-matoes have to travel far and are never very cheap. No butcher comes to the remoter parts of the parish.

[2] Richard Hoggart, *The Uses of Literacy* (London 1957).

desirable it is and the manner in which to raise their standards in every sector of their life. In towns, the 'keeping-up-with-the-Joneses' competition takes the form of complete moves up. If a young couple buy a new house, the chances are high that they also buy towels with pictures on, soft lavatory paper and modern Christmas cards; have a certain kind of crockery, shape of cutlery, style of decoration, and hope to go abroad for their holidays. If they cannot go that far up, and move into a flat, they will live in a style that more or less goes with the flat; not because they restrict their ideals to what is 'suitable to a flat', but because they tend to have a system of priorities. They want carpets – but not at the cost of having no holiday at all. They want an all-round if small improvement on their parents' way of life: say a motor-bike; an electric stove that works; adequate crockery, mats on top of the linoleum and so on. This is a great over-simplification of the varieties of ways of life people live in the towns, and an exaggeration of those people's logic, but I think it points to a real contrast between town and Llan patterns of spending. I cannot tell how much of what I say of Llan here is also true of other rural areas. The 'keeping-up-with-the-Joneses' competition has hardly reach Llan, at least; and only in certain show items – unevenly. There is not widespread, yet, the idea of striving for complete 'other ways of life'. Calls on the housewife's purse are made plainly through catalogues of goods she can buy through the post. A woman bought a new kitchen cabinet for £30 and continued to cook over a coal fire. When it came to buying an electric stove, she had a false idea of her own poverty and somehow, the purchase of the kitchen cabinet 'on the club' was not taken into account as part of the expenses of daily life. It is not safe to assume, as it would be in an English town, when one sees a large electric mixer in the kitchen, that there will be a coffee percolator and carpets in the lounge, or even that there will be a lounge.

This general picture of rather erratic expenditure is less true of farmers than it is of the rest of the population. The farmers save money more than do others. It is easier for farmers than for other people to save, firstly, because they get money in bulk sums and secondly, because if they continue to farm they are obliged to invest: in a good car, in new stock, in implements and so on. However, as I explain in Chapter Four, the distinction between farmers and non-farmers is not nearly so clear in North Wales as in English country districts and this applies to the pattern of spending as to other things.

But the fact that Llan people assume that they are poorer than they are is mainly revealed by their opinion of the wealth of other people. One of my neighbours found it hard to believe that the Assistance rates are the same in London as they are in Llan. Many Welsh Nationalist voters had a feeling, not generally put into words but which emerged from discussions, that Englishmen were paid more for the same job and generally got a better deal all round.

The following figures give some idea of the actual poverty of Wales as compared with the rest of Britain.

In June 1959 the percentage of unemployed in Wales was 3·4 whilst in Great Britain the figure was 1·9. In 1951 the percentage of unemployed in North West Wales was 2·7 whilst in England and Wales the figure was 0·9.[1]

In 1950 (Census of Distribution) the amount spent in retail shops per head of the population in England was £120, in Wales £95, in Merioneth £86. (These figures include money spent in shops by visitors on holiday; they omit money spent buying through the post, which is widespread in all rural areas of Great Britain.)

Average Earnings from Wages and Salaries – Principal Source of Income[2] £s per annum

	1949–50	*1954–55*	% *Increase*
England	346·97	475·25	37·0
Wales	331·04	462·30	39·7
Merioneth	287·17	380·28	32·4
Westmorland[3]	307·98	405·71	31·7

The Welsh are poorer than the English generally, then, but whilst Llan people, in what they say to each other try to appear individually richer than they are, from what they do and the

[1] S. Jones and G. P. Smith *Employment and Unemployment in North-West Wales* (Bangor 1960) (*vide* note, page 13).

[2] Commissioner of Inland Revenue Annual Returns, Survey of Incomes.

[3] Figures for this county are included for comparison.

way they live as well as from their opinions of other people, it is clear that they regard themselves, as a group, as poorer than they really are.

It is against this background that the place of the English in Llan thought should be seen.

The explanation to the paradoxes I noticed in Llan life, the key to understanding Llan people, and therefore the main theme of this book, is the anti-English feeling of Welsh-speaking people. Apart from the fact that it disguises under its surface other antagonisms, this feeling, taken at its face value, exists on two levels. The first level is the complex feeling Llan people have towards English people as a result of their actual social relations with English individuals. The second level is the feeling which North Welsh people as a whole have towards England as an impersonal outside force, governing them, imposing a foreign tongue on them, and sending minions in the form of officials to impose its rules. Outside of this chapter, it is the second level of anti-English feeling to which I refer in this book. This second level of feeling I shall call the partisan feeling because it turns the North Welsh people into partisans, fighting for their Welshness and it is not ambiguous. You are either Welsh and in that case in the fight; or you are trying to be English in which case you are on the other side.

The first, personal, level of anti-English feeling I shall describe as though it were unanimous and unambiguous, but it is not so in fact, because different individuals have different relations with the English individuals they meet – and some of these relations, inevitably, are close and friendly. Such differences are ignored in order to simplify the description of the social structure of the parish with which this and the following chapters are concerned. However, it should be borne in mind that the ambiguity and lack of unanimity in this first level of anti-English feeling make it milder than the second level. Personal relationships mitigate the anti-English feeling on the first level. For most of the village, Mrs. X may be just another 'saesnes' (Englishwoman); to some she is a good friend and neighbour. For most of the village, Mr. Vaughan is just the English landlord; to some he is a man who has done them a good turn.

A stereotype of the English, as representatives of the abstraction 'ruling England', is at the root of many of the attitudes generally held in North Wales, and is, therefore, impervious to quick adjustment. Adjustment is not demanded by many of the English people who are seen regularly in Llan, since for most people they fit the stereotype. The lack of class divisions in Welsh society itself, described for Llan in Chapter Three, is due partly to the anglicization of the upper strata of Welsh society and partly to the fact that the rulers of Wales have long been English corporations and English-speaking individuals. The English take the place of the upper, upper-middle or ruling class, and nationalism is the dress in which class antagonisms are expressed. The stereotype which Llan people have of English people as snobbish, rich and lacking in understanding, was formed in pre-war days when most of the English they saw were powerful and rich.[1] This type of English person still has enough power over the lives of the Llan people and the people of North Wales generally to reinforce the stereotype.

There are two main estates in Llan, that of Mr. Vaughan called Plas and that of Colonel Forde called Cwmparc. Colonel Forde is the Master of the Hounds, and organizes and leads the hunt which, as in some other mountainous districts, is pursued on foot. Cwmparc Estate is regarded in some ways as the true manor or big house of the district, though much of the estate lies in a neighbouring parish and although the two Cwmparc families are much poorer than the Plas family. Rents of farms have not increased much in the last fifty years; wartime and post-war farming methods have demanded buildings in good order. Expenses have been great for the main Cwmparc family since the war, whilst their real income has decreased. This impoverishment has brought them nearer to Llan people.

The Plas family do not see themselves quite so much in the manorial role. Percy Vaughan, the present landlord, is a publisher and he gets substantial income from his work in that profession, He is more interested in the appearance of the estate than in the social life of its inhabitants. He deals through an

---

[1] 'In Wales . . . for long periods of its history, English and Welsh have been almost synonymous with landlord and tenant or capital and labour.' R. Frankenberg, *Village on the Border* (London 1957).

agent, a method of procedure which is not popular since its results in his tenants receiving impersonal typewritten notices and experiencing long delays. He has bought a great deal of land since he inherited the Plas estate, and let cottages that have become empty to English intellectuals who could afford to spend on their holiday houses more than working people in Llan can afford to spend on their homes.

The Cwmparc families know every villager by his or her Christian name and recognize them in the street. Colonel Forde drinks and plays darts with local people. The Plas family probably know everyone too, but they act as though they do not, and are remote from the life of the village. The Cwmparc family farm and always have done, whilst the Plas family seem to have no connection with work or dirt. The present occupant of the Cwmparc Estate is addressed familiarly as 'Colonel' whilst the Plas man is always addressed as Mr. Vaughan.

Nevertheless, both families, though in fact two branches of one very old Welsh family, are regarded as English and both families own a lot of land and many houses. The Cwmparc people speak a kind of broken Welsh, the Plas people speak no Welsh.[1] On shearing day at Cwmparc, the Colonel does not eat with the workers, who are mostly other farmers, and I have heard it said of the annual parties given by Plas for the village children that 'the children stand outside the gate until exactly 3.30 when they are let in, and are ushered out at exactly 4.30 to wait in the road for their parents'. In fact this impression was created by the necessity for some 'marshalling' to give tea and presents to a substantial number of children; but some Llan people have seen the organization of the party as an example of Plas people's aloofness. Another example is the saying, significant if not quite serious, that some Llan people vote Conservative because the Plas people support Labour and so Labour must be the wrong party for ordinary people to vote for. Cwmparc people, as well as having a certain place in village life, also move in 'county' circles unknown to the village, while the Plas people move in intellectual, business and political circles which centre mainly in London.

[1] However, it is interesting to note that the grandchildren of Mr. Vaughan and Colonel Forde's daughter are learning Welsh.

On the whole, then, for most people most of the time, these families of Welsh gentry, because they are regarded as English, reinforce the stereotype which North Welsh people have of English people, as do the quarry-owners and managers, the people with the top jobs in the Electricity Board, and the factory, and other English people who make money in Wales. But there are three other groups of English people who have made their appearance in Llan since the war; the passing-through tourists, the climbers and the intellectuals.

First there are the tourists. These stop for teas, postcards, snapshots of the mountains and trains to the top of Snowdon, and are the 'mugs' that tourists are everywhere to native populations. Their cars clutter up the roads, their money is welcomed. Occasionally some Liverpudlians have a drink in one of the pubs, get merry and start to sing old-fashioned English popular songs. Then the locals may be annoyed if they had hoped for serious singing; may go elsewhere or try to out-sing the visitors if they feel belligerent; or may strike up a brief friendship and join in. But these passing tourists make no impression. Little is learnt about them or from them. They probably speak with a Yorkshire or Lancashire accent – they are obviously not the 'big people'. But they have new cars, they are on holiday and so they must have money to throw about. Very few Llan people go away for holidays.

Secondly, there are the climbers. Before the war, climbers were rarely working-class; now they often are, and this breaks down the stereotype to a certain extent. On the other hand, poor or rich, climbers are obviously crazy.

'Fancy climbing Snowdon for fun and then feeling proud of it when Will Pritchard, skinny, 45 and no hero, toils up Snowdon every day to dig ditches and wouldn't bother to mention it except as one disadvantage of his present job; and when old Jos Jones has been walking up that steep pipeline going up Mynydd Mawr to test the level of the water for the power station every day for many years. These English people must have very easy jobs to come and walk about mountains for the fun of it.'

The third post-war group which has made its appearance in Llan is the group of intellectuals, and it is this group which makes Llan different from most of the rest of North Wales.

Summer visitors to Llan are not builders from Manchester or factory hands from Liverpool, or shopkeepers from Bootle – people who would tell you in the pub how much they were earning and what they meant to do with the money. They are professors, lecturers, painters, authors and doctors. Most of them own or rent cottages on the Llan mountain slopes and come to the parish for the long University holidays, year after year. With them and around them move one or two well-read penniless eccentrics, and the whole group, especially its lower ranks, causes much amusement and food for talk in the parish. Llan is sometimes described as the Greenwich Village of Wales. In the summer of 1959, the following remarks were overheard in the public house in Dinas: 'My dear, it's *just* like Hampstead.' 'No, it's not at all surprising we met them here. Simply everyone comes to Llan.'

How did the English regulars get here? Most of them have come through Vaughan, the owner of the Plas Estate. Percy Vaughan, now over 80, is well known as a publisher, his wife is an author, and they move in intellectual circles which centre in London. Few of the regulars were introduced to the district directly by Vaughan, but the push that brought them here emanated from him originally; and they are the kind of people he wants. He has stated publicly about the abandoned cottages which he lets: 'We have been very careful of the occupants. They are mostly of the intelligentsia.'

Vaughan's son-in-law introduced one of the most influential of them, Edward Lewis, and by speaking of Lewis I can describe the peculiar flavour of our group of visitors. Lewis was born in Southern England and read history at Cambridge during the war. In 1949 he came to Llan with his wife and one child and started sheep-farming on a small mountain farm. In the next ten years they had four more children, gradually built up their flock and expanded the farm and won the affection and respect of most of their neighbours. They spent quite a lot of money doing it. Nevertheless, for Llan, this is a very unusual story. Other Englishmen have tried to farm in Llan and the district, have started with capital and have failed, gone bankrupt or moved or both. Unlike them, say the Llan farmers, Edward listened to his neighbours' advice, learnt from them, drank with them, gathered, sheared and dipped sheep with them and treated everyone alike with courtesy and generosity.

Other English came, similarly intent on going back to the land. But North Wales beat them. They had firm ideas on how to make money; they could not manage to mix easily and equally with the Welshmen; their wives could not bear the damp, crude, isolated cottages. To farm in the district, a man must either have the constant, daily co-operation of his fellow farmers, or he must have a very large sum of money behind him. The land is so poor that, for the average-sized farm, it is not economical for one farmer to own all the implements needed to farm it. As explained in Chapter Four farm implements are shared, as is the skilled labour of the farmers, at times when a lot of work must be done quickly – as at shearing time. An outsider who wishes to farm in the district and who cannot act as an equal towards his fellow men, will in time forfeit the right to the help which he needs in order to succeed. If he wishes to be independent, he has to invest very heavily. So that to succeed, the kind of outsiders who came needed, firstly, some capital because they could not live on as low a standard as Llan people do and they were bound to make mistakes; secondly, a capacity to learn humbly from others about the economy and methods of farming in North Wales; and thirdly, and most important of all, the ability to mix with Welsh people as an equal. The few who tried failed. But they helped to initiate a strange competition among the regulars, whether holiday-makers or residents.

A comparison with a super-brow will help me to explain. A low-brow reads comics, likes Elvis Presley, gangster films and Westerns; a high-brow likes Bach, French and Japanese films; a superbrow, once a high-brow, loathes his fellow high-brows so much, particularly since they include many who pretend to like Bach, French and Japanese films, that if he does not quite take to reading comics, he certainly enthuses over James Dean, Westerns and gangster films.

There is something similar in the competition that takes place amongst the English regulars in Llan. So anxious are they not to fit into the Welsh stereotype of the English as arrogant snobs that they take pains to mingle with the locals, drink more beer than they would do at home, are beginning to talk of going poaching, and maintain that they have been coming here for such a long time that they do not count as visitors and indeed are practically villagers. I am not sure any of the people in question would like to be regarded as Welsh people or as country people in their English home towns. But like those tourists everywhere who want to disassociate themselves from their fellow tourists; like those who will not buy the red MG they would like because of the people who do buy red MG's, like the foreign nobles who in Italy, Greece and Ireland have at various times joined rebel bands, our English visitors try, but never wholeheartedly enough, to be part of Welsh society. And by doing this they hope to gain prestige in the 'in-group' which they in fact wish to join, the group of 'real' regulars.

Thus the beauty of Llan, its lack of fame as a holiday resort and the fact that its largest landlord moves in intellectual circles, have given the Llan population an interesting summer adornment and caused Llan people to modify slightly their stereotype of an Englishman. The extent to which the English intellectuals who regularly visit Llan have succeeded in their efforts to break up the Welsh stereotype of the English is something that is difficult to gauge. As I have explained above, the regulars are not completely sincere or wholehearted in their endeavours to 'become one of the locals': they try to do so largely to win points in a competition among themselves. And however much they drink, swear, wear old clothes, play darts, talk about poaching, and know the correct names of places and people, the regulars are wealthy by comparison with Llan people, clearly have good jobs and seem to have little to do except watch the Llan people. By some their confidence is read as a sign of typically English arrogance; their frequent careless-ness or generosity with money is read as a sign of typically English wealth. They modify the stereotype of the English which Llan people have; they introduce a 'crazy' side to the picture so that one hears not only of 'bloody Saxons' but also of 'mad English'; but they do nothing to change the Llan people's con-viction that the English are a rich people and the Welsh are a poor one. Indeed, as I have explained above, it would take great changes to upset radically the stereotype Llan people have of the English and of 'England' as an abstraction because upon it depends so many of their attitudes; in it are included so many of their antagonisms and conflicts; and around it have grown up so many of their modes of behaviour. The stereotype can confront English people seen as modest, charming and unassuming and survive the contact unscathed.

CHAPTER THREE

PRESTIGE LADDERS

THE Act of Union between England and Wales enacted by Henry VIII in 1535, which was intended to 'extirp' all the 'sinister usages' by which the Welsh differed from the English, imposed English laws of inheritance upon Wales and banned from office any person who used the Welsh language.

'A division now appeared in the national life, an ever-widening breach separating the gentry from the common people. The crystallization of landlordism into a social system and the anglicization of the upper classes proceeded simultaneously. Becoming increasingly alienated from its traditions and heritage, the Welsh aristocratic class renounced the duties and obligations which for time out of mind it had discharged and honoured. The change, though gradual, was completed by the end of the eighteenth century.'[1]

In Llan the 'gentry' are anglicized and remote from the common people. They belong to old Welsh families of just the type which Jarman describes. The largest landowner, Percy Vaughan, was born in the district and his father was born in the parish, but he does not speak Welsh. Apart from the fact that the big landlords are counted by Llan people as English, it is interesting to see that the process described by Jarman continues today and, to a certain extent, groups in North Welsh society which wish to rise in status, borrow English manners and modes of dress and display conspicuously their knowledge of the English language. Limits are set to this tendency by self-conscious Welsh Nationalism on the part of many with 'middle-class' occupations, the strength of the local tradition, and local opposition. For those who move away to England, this trend is

[1] A. O. H. Jarman, *The Historical Basis of Welsh Nationalism* (Cardiff 1950).

of no significance once they are in England, because when there they are obliged to be fairly English in these outward respects. For those who work in the parish, it is almost impossible to be wholeheartedly anglicized. The trend is most clearly seen among those who go to work in a neighbouring town in a white-collar job.

So a consideration of social stratification in the parish must begin with a reminder that the Welsh/English opposition gives shape to much of the grouping.

At the top of the social hierarchy in Llan stand the two families of gentry: the Plas Estate family, comprising Percy Vaughan, his wife, his daughter, son-in-law and grand-children, and the Cwmparc Estate family, comprising Colonel Forde, his wife, his daughter and his two aunts.

There are various ways of defining the social position of any particular group. Some sociologists are guided by where other people would place that group. A consensus of public opinion in Llan would place the Plas and Cwmparc people at the apex of the hierarchy.

Some sociologists are guided by some objective material criteria in the way of life of the group and by these, the Plas and Cwmparc people would be placed at the top of the hier-archy. Their incomes are high;[1] their children go to boarding-schools, their houses are large and they have domestic help liv-ing in.

Some sociologists and economists are guided by the Marxist definition of class and place people by another objective material criterion; according to their relationship to the means of production. The position of landlord gives Mr. Vaughan and Colonel Forde power over people's lives. They own the means of production of many workers; they are of the ruling class; and they qualify to top the hierarchy by this definition too. Thus the main current methods of division into social classes have the same result of putting clearly at the top these two families.

Beneath this apex, how are Llan people stratified? In many

[1] Nevertheless, there is probably at least one farmer in the parish with a higher income than the Cwmparc family, although I have no concrete evidence of this.

parts of rural Great Britain, the next layer in the hierarchy would be the farmers, forming a distinct social group, in some places equivalent socially to businessmen.[1] But, as explained in Chapter Four, this is not the case in Llan and farmers must be counted as existing on the same social stratum as manual workers. The situation is changing; the economic position of farmers has been improving steadily since 1939 and in time this economic change will affect their social position. But there is always a time-lag to such developments and the social change has not yet been effected.[2]

Eighty-six per cent of Llan's Welsh working population work in occupations which could be described as manual labour and these occupations vary very little in the amount of prestige they bring to those who practise them. Because there is pride in local tradition, and in Welshness, when a man works with his hands he gains prestige of a kind. To do so is not a proof of stupidity. Everyone may not know that Giotto was a shepherd, but everyone does know that many famous Welsh poets were and are shepherds. Those who work with their hands maintain links with the hard old way of life and thus gain prestige on the scale where marks are given for Welshness. But a man does not have to be a manual worker to climb this ladder. Occupation is not the criterion by which prestige of this kind is gained.

The Welsh group of white-collared workers comprises:

8 clerks
8 shopkeepers and shop assistants
4 teachers
1 nurse
1 apprentice surveyor

[1] 'The English labourer and his employer are drawn from two different classes in the social scale, whereas in Wales it might be said that as a general rule there does not exist that class cleavage between the farmer and the labourer.' *The Report of the Welsh Land Inquiry, Rural* (London 1914).

[2] Because of this time-lag I believe that while an economic criterion such as the relation to the means of production might well be the most useful one for describing social stratification historically, or describing changes which take place over time, the most useful criteria for the study of a present-day community are where people place a particular group, and that group's way of life.

1 insurance agent
2 salesmen
1 W.E.A. lecturer

It is necessary for all members of this group to wear English styles of clothing, that is to say clothes more modern and colourful than most other parishioners wear[1] (a literally 'white' collar is no longer a must), and to be able to read and speak English well. To climb the prestige ladder which exists commonly for all of Great Britain, it is necessary to have a white-collar job and to be able to speak and read English well; and so each holder of a white-collar job in Llan gains prestige on this ladder by virtue of his occupation. He could be 'somebody' elsewhere than in Llan.

Speaking good English and being accredited with social superiority are closely connected. When a Welsh-speaking person telephones the hospital to ask after a sick relative and cannot understand clearly what is said because the ward sister speaks English, he feels inferior. So does he when he feels ill but cannot explain quite what he feels like to the English doctor; or when he has to ask someone else to fill in a form for him because he is not sure about the big words in English. Only five of the Welsh people in Llan can speak no English,[2] but many others are not happy when speaking English. Many do not understand English slang, English jokes, or archaic or rarely used words such as 'merry', official language such as 'forward' when it means 'send' as in 'forward to this office'. Dialects and

[1] Young manual workers may be seen wearing trousers and jackets for work which their fathers wore fifty years ago, patched jeans, old bits of army battledress, patched wellingtons or two pairs of trousers one on top of the other, worn together in the hope that the holes in one will not coincide with the holes in the other.

[2] This was written in 1959. In the 1951 Census, 93 of the full civil parish of Llan's (see Sketch Map 1) population of 543 returned themselves as 'speaking Welsh only'. The population of the part of Llan I am writing about was 346 in 1959. The idea of advantages thought to be derived from pretending not to know things, described in Chapter Eight, operates here and some people will have exaggerated their ignorance of the English language when completing the census forms. If they cannot understand the official language, they cannot be expected to comply with official regulations.

local accents are especially difficult for those to whom English is a second language.

It is humiliating for a man to feel inadequate on many of the important occasions in his life: prize-giving at his daughter's school; answering a summons in court; or calling a doctor.[1] Court cases are heard in English and interpreters only occasionally allowed. The chairmen of the benches in the two magistrates' courts nearest to Llan are English and cases are heard in English before them, witnesses being allowed to give evidence in Welsh if they prove they cannot speak English reasonably well. Ellis Cae Du, who is 29 years of age, pleaded guilty when he meant to plead not guilty to a motoring offence in 1957 and was too embarrassed at his lack of English and too inarticulate in that language to explain his error. He preferred to take the consequences of the mistake than to try to explain anything in English, show his inferior education or risk being laughed at over the mistake.[2] People ask me to write official letters for them and the practice of asking someone else to write such letters is not uncommon.

Some few people will try to avoid being found in circumstances where they have to submit to the indignity of feeling inferior in what is, after all, their home country. They refuse to see the doctor, never go to official gatherings, even fail to claim benefits due to them. Others insist on having an interpreter in court, and make sure they find a Welsh doctor and dentist. To others, this is too much trouble – they can manage in English and they do their best. To others, to ask for an interpreter, or look for a Welsh doctor, is to admit that they cannot speak English and so they will carry on in English, saying as little as possible.

If speaking poor English makes a man inferior, speaking good

[1] '. . . a man with little command over English is caused a certain amount of distress and embarrassment both during the stage when he completes the Army Form and, later, when he is taking the Army Group Test'. Report of the Welsh National Serviceman Committee, 3rd Memorandum of the Council for Wales and Monmouthshire, 1957.

[2] Side by side with this real embarrassment about lack of English is the sophisticated use of the embarrassment by others. Thus some young men with excellent English pretend to be unable to speak English in court in order to gain time when answering questions. See also footnote 1 over.

English makes him superior and I think it is true to say that no one in Llan speaks fluent English without feeling at least a little better than those who cannot do so. English people do not feel that their use of the English language makes them superior and most of them are unaware that social superiority and the English language are associated in North Wales. Indeed, most English people are surprised to hear Welsh spoken at all when they first visit North Wales, and admire Welsh people for their bilingualism. It is Welsh-speaking people who think of the English language in this way.

Thus the white-collared workers in Llan gain prestige because they are doing jobs which would give prestige anywhere in Great Britain and because to have those jobs they should and almost certainly do speak English more correctly and fluently than most other people in their community.

What breaks up this award of prestige by virtue of occupation and linguistic ability is the opposing prestige ladder I have mentioned, on which a person climbs higher by being more Welsh than others. The extent to which the white-collared workers in Llan take advantage of their ability to qualify for 'English prestige' depends upon their vulnerability to demands that they should succeed in obtaining 'Welsh prestige'. Factors which affect this vulnerability are age, whether or not they work outside the parish, and to a slight extent which part of the parish they live in.

The older a man is, the more he remembers of Wales before the war and the national planning it necessitated had altered its economy, and before cinemas, radios, transport and National Service had made any appreciable impression on its culture. The group of people who matter to an old man and whose opinions most influence him tend to be old themselves. Few of them had opportunities to rise on the English prestige ladder; to them Welshness is what counts and a white-collared worker of their generation risks losing a lot if he rejects their values for English values.

The younger a man is, the more likely he is to have been called up to serve in the British forces, to go to the cinema, and generally to be influenced by modern things. Not only has a young man more opportunity to climb the English ladder and

35

less to lose by doing so than has and does an older man, but the elements of the new culture, the adoption of which goes with climbing the English ladder, are elements more likely to appeal to a young man than to an old man.

Thus age affects the vulnerability of a white-collared worker to demands that he should succeed on the Welsh prestige ladder and it is partly for this reason, that one of the salesmen, the headmaster of Dinas school, the proprietor of the post office in Dinas, the W.E.A. lecturer and the nurse have not taken advantage of the chances offered to them by the nature of their jobs to climb the English prestige ladder. The headmaster's father was a quarrymen, both his pairs of grandparents farmed in the parish. The proprietor of the post office in Dinas was brought up on a farm by his widowed mother and had a child-hood of great hardship. His children have all left the parish and started to climb the English prestige ladder; one son is the manager of a large shop, another is an engineer, and the other son is a doctor. But Gwyn, although proud of his children, himself sticks to the old ways. The nurse, who worked in English cities in her youth, similarly refrains from taking ad-vantage of her status, and on a Women's Institute outing, far from trying to impress the English members of the W.I. who were present, sat in the bus with a headscarf round her grey hair, vigorously leading the singing of favourite Welsh songs and hymns. In the same way, one of the salesmen and the W.E.A. lecturer have 'stayed Welsh' and their age is partly responsible for this.

But the second of the factors I listed above also affects the headmaster of Dinas school and the proprietor of the post office and makes it even more difficult for them to take advantage of their possible positions on the English prestige ladder: that is the fact that their work is in the parish.

The W.E.A. lecturer and the nurse could 'put on airs' at work since they work outside the parish and had they started to do so at work they would then have become divorced from the very Welsh life of the parish. But the headmaster and post-master pass their days in the parish of Llan itself and thus are exposed all day long to the local pressures to conform to the Welsh pattern.

The third factor which may make a white-collared worker give others and hope to receive himself Welsh rather than English prestige is the part of the parish in which he lives. Each part of the parish has a tradition of its own, and the part of the parish in which a person lives affects his social position or social aspirations. Dinas is the neat, picturesque centrepiece of the parish. The houses in Dinas are either owned by Vaughan and have been modernized by him so as to have water and sanitation or are owned by the Council, in which case they have baths as well as lavatories. All but three of the white-collared workers of Llan who work outside the district live in Dinas, and from their point of view the Council houses are the best places to live in because they are the most modern houses in the parish. The rents of the Council houses are higher than those of other houses in the parish and the snob value of living in a Council house in Llan is an interesting reversal of the usual association of Council house tenancy with low social standing.

A person living in Pensarn or Aber, both on roads out of Llan, breathes in a very different atmosphere from that of Dinas. Pensarn is an untidy corner of the parish scattered with hens, geese, sheds, motor-cycles and bits of old machinery. Most of its inhabitants own their own houses and have neither baths nor lavatories. Aber is high up, remote, with no buses. It is not worth trying to dress up for either place, and the kind of people who live in them do not want to, anyway. Carmel is the village in the Llan mountains which was built around a slate quarry in 1865 and which has declined considerably since the quarry was closed in 1930. The arch at the entrance to the Carmel road stopped loaded lorries from entering it; no public transport runs along the road, and it leads to nowhere but Carmel. Until the end of the war there were very few cars in Carmel and the place was very isolated. Now all the farmers there have cars and are quite prosperous, but the influence of the past is strongly felt. Aber is really a dying community; Carmel is still sufficiently populated to have a community which thinks it is dying. The chapel is very influential in Carmel; the Sunday school there is attended by more adults than children; the Welsh Nationalist vote there is high. There is one young clerical worker, Cledwyn, who works outside the parish but lives in Carmel. He has been brought up amongst farmers with their backs to the mountain, their eyes on the dead slate quarry and their memories full of Carmel with a population three times its present size. Cledwyn's office job outside the parish cuts him off from parish life. But the social environment in which he grew up has made its impression on him and he votes Welsh Nationalist; although in the work he is doing he is climbing the English prestige ladder, he tries to do it in a Welsh way.

This influence of the local social environment must be seen as more social than geographical, although both elements are present. To a large extent people choose to live in the parts of the parish in which they do live. People who live in Pensarn and who wish to climb the English ladder tend to move to a Council house in Dinas sooner or later. Their regard for the 'old life' has a lot to do with Cledwyn's parents living in Carmel and therefore with his views on status.

People's views on life work on their children partly through the place in which they choose to live and bring up their children. In the same way an African child brought up in a town is affected by the slum life around him and the values of the people in it; and this effect is a result of his parents' or grandparents' decision to move to the town and it operates on him together with the influence of the values his parents must have to have made the move towards the town, or to have stayed there.

The individuals I have described so far in this chapter have been white-collared workers who, because of their age, and sometimes because they work in the parish, behave in ways which gain them Welsh rather than English prestige: people to whom the respect of Welsh-speaking people is more important than the knowledge that their jobs could put them in 'a class apart'. In Cledwyn's case, the part of the parish in which he lives is one of the factors making him wish for Welsh prestige, although his other circumstances: being young, a clerical worker, and working outside the parish, result in him being placed by others on the English ladder. There are others like Cledwyn for whom the influences they are exposed to are conflicting. Most tradesmen in the district are dependent for their living on the English visitors in the summer and on the Welsh manual workers in the winter, and some of these, married and of middling age, are open to two sets of pressures. They are not old enough to be irrevocably Welsh and if for other reasons they are attracted to the climbers, tourists and intellectuals, they will walk and talk briskly with an air of authority, like town men; try to keep abreast of current affairs, be ready to pass opinions on any topic; dress in the English style; in short, strive to climb the English prestige ladder. But in the winter months, not young enough to join the anglicized groups of teenagers who drink coffee in the towns, or the bachelor groups who frequent the Sunday clubs,[1] they are left to and depend for their livelihood on groups of local cap-wearing Welsh-speaking people. They will then be obliged to pay some homage to Welsh ways, to laugh at the English and try to achieve status on the Welsh ladder. They are thus straddled between the two ladders in a most uncomfortable, indeed almost impossible fashion; since to be thoroughly Welsh it is necessary to be the opposite of English (i.e. act in ways opposite to what is thought to be typical English behaviour, that is to be slow in speech and movement; undistinguished in dress and unforthcoming in opinion; especially opinion on matters of world affairs). Their anglicized mannerisms in combination with the work they do result in their being placed by others firmly on a low rung of the English prestige ladder.

This idea of English manners held by North Welsh people sounds so much like English country people's ideas of English town people that I should like to repeat here what I have said already; that is, that the country versus town feeling is a large and important part of the Welsh versus English feeling but is seen by the people for the most part in terms of Welsh versus English. Ideal nationality takes the place of class and locality. Town/country, and upper-class/working-class antagonisms are forced into the mould, suffering some distortion in the process. Thus 'towny' town inhabitants are criticized on the grounds that they are anglicized rather than that they are

[1] Drinking clubs which thrive because the pubs are closed in Wales on Sundays.

'towny' and class affiliations are sometimes blurred by 'Welsh-ness'.

The ambiguous position of such tradesmen as I have been describing above is sometimes reflected in the behaviour of their children. One such child in Llan is Bob. Bob works as a clerk outside the parish. He stayed at school long enough to take the G.C.E. and he dresses in the English style. But he is not quite sure that it is the English ladder he wishes to climb. He collects pieces of old motor-cycles in his spare time, makes them up into machines and sells them and, in connection with this hobby, meets manual labourers of the district on an equal basis, and gets as dirty as they do. He is very friendly with the lads who work in the parish, and he poaches.

Bob's position on the cross-roads is partly a reflection of his father's ambiguous social position; partly a personal reaction against his parents' unequivocal desire that he should mount the English ladder; and partly a wavering he shares with all the youngsters of the parish. They are all attracted by much of the English way of life (and by English I here mean Anglo-American). They want to learn to jive; they like to go to the cinema; they listen to popular record programmes on the radio; they like to wear 'teen-age' clothes. But they all feel the pull of the Welsh culture; are proud of their own language and generally prefer to speak Welsh to English. I asked one girl of 17 what she hoped to do when she left school and she replied:

'Oh, I'd like to get a job in London for a year or two and then come back here and marry a farmer.' (By farmer, she meant farmer or smallholder as I use the terms.) Another girl of 14 said she wanted to do something with animals. Both these girls have pictures of American film stars pinned round the walls of their bedrooms. Both of them wish to live out most of or all their lives in Llan parish. Whether they will do so or not remains to be seen.[1] It is interesting to note that they say now that they will stay in Llan, and they are neither unintelligent nor untypical of their age-group, although others of that group

---

[1] This was written in 1959. In 1962 the first girl had spent two years in London and had returned to Llan; the second girl was working on a farm in Llan.

say, as a lot of teenagers tend to do everywhere, that they want to go away and never come back.

A little older than the teenage group mentioned in the preceding paragraph are the shop assistants and most of the office-workers in the list of occupations; and it is this latter group, young and working outside the parish in clean jobs, who most successfully resist local pressures and are becoming anglicized. The girls respond to advice in the women's journals that pale lipstick is the vogue; they try to avoid wearing wellington boots; they persuade their parents to buy television sets; they hope to marry 'rich Englishmen'; they cultivate 'good' English accents and may even speak English amongst themselves occasionally – in a café in town, for instance. The boys do not go poaching, walk in a brisk, uncountrified fashion, buy or hope to buy good cars, the insides of which they will not tinker about with, and hold themselves aloof from the gang of youths in the village.

Another group of white-collared workers who, like the tradesmen of middling age and the teenagers, are particularly exposed to conflicting influences, are those professional workers who do not leave Wales. Their spell at a University and the universal standing of their jobs has anglicized them; but the Welsh culture often has an appeal to them based on an intellectual appreciation of its value. They are often well informed about Welsh history and culture and may have chosen to stay in North Wales because of their affection for Wales and Welsh people and things. Even if their motive were simply to take advantage of the existence of good jobs which they could do, it is hard for them to live in North Wales, especially those of them who live in the countryside, without paying some tribute to Welsh ways. But though aware of conflicting influences, Welsh-speaking professional workers have almost no choice: they are high up on the English prestige ladder.

By a prestige ladder I mean a consensus of public opinion which gives respect to different individuals in different degrees. When I speak of the English prestige ladder I mean that the bulk of people in Great Britain give more respect to a doctor than to a teacher; more to a teacher than to a clerk; more to a clerk than to a welder; and more to a welder than to a dustman.

I refer to this ladder of jobs, placed one above the other, because a good deal of work has been done on it: it has been found that people's occupations are a relatively simple and effective sign by which they can be and are graded; and comparisons have been made between the way occupations are graded in Great Britain, New Zealand and the U.S.A. So a doctor, in the act of becoming a doctor, climbs high upon the English prestige ladder: that is he takes a job which gives him a certain amount of prestige in the English value system; and having decided on that profession and succeeded in reaching it, automatically and irrevocably receives the degree of prestige which other people do accord to doctors. I have said above that he has almost no choice: a place is ascribed to him by most people and there is little he can do to alter it. If this is so with a doctor or minister then, it may be argued, it must be the case with the school teacher, nurse, postmaster, W.E.A. lecturer and other white-collared workers of Llan whom I described earlier in this chapter. But their case is not quite the same. I wrote about these white-collared workers that the strength of local values was such that they could opt out of the English prestige system. And whilst it is true that a certain amount of prestige, no more and no less, is ascribed in the English system to people holding their jobs, that ascription of prestige to a certain job is only half the story of the English status system, which does not fully operate unless a corresponding way of life is followed. To study status systems as they operate in a particular social situation, it is necessary to look at the way of life of the individual concerned, that is his mannerisms, speech, clothes and way of spending money, as well as at his job. In Llan it is possible to be a Welsh white-collared worker and not 'be a nob'; not cut oneself off from manual workers in the ways expected of white-collared workers in English society. In the same way, in Llan, farmers are not a separate social group because they do not behave and particularly do not spend money in ways appreciably different from other manual workers. But there are certain rungs high up on the English prestige ladder which claim the complete occupant almost irrevocably and these include the rungs occupied by professional workers. There is no elasticity in these high reaches. The period of training required for the professions involves a long absence from 'home' people and things; it involves the acquisition of a new language, a new vocabulary, new methods of thinking and expression which once learnt cannot be forgotten. The practice of a profession continues this process of estrangement from others: the professional worker, as minister, doctor, lawyer or high-grade Civil Servant, is placed in a role which makes his relations with other people special and unequal. Thus the professional worker can rarely opt out of the English prestige system. What often happens is that he regrets his estrangement when it is too late. In North Wales, where the culture he leaves behind is rich and beautiful, his regrets may be powerful and may cause him to start thinking consciously of himself as Welsh. He may try to 'be Welsh' by walking and dressing and arranging his home in an unpretentious way. More often he approaches 'being Welsh' from the top: advocates the teaching of science in the Welsh language; agitates for more Welsh radio programmes; eschews the use of the countless English words which, disguised by Welsh pronunciation, have found their way into colloquial Welsh; is politically active in the nationalist cause and by his very conscious affiliation to the Welsh life, goes a step farther in cutting himself off from it.

It is my contention in this chapter that in rural North Wales there are two status systems, corresponding to two sets of values: the English and the Welsh; and I have referred to opposing prestige ladders. The idea of a ladder suits the English system because sociologists have found, by means of questionnaires, that people do grade jobs, one on top of the other, as more or less prestige-giving. The Welsh system is not so clearly hierarchical because there is no one criterion by which a man is more or less Welsh. It is not a simple case of shepherds being at the top and quarrymen a bit farther down, with 'Welsh' school teachers being fairly near the bottom. Nor is participation in the world of Welsh music and poetry the simple criterion: which would put a 'bardd' at the top, a harpist or a good singer next, a man with a wide knowledge of Welsh literature next, and so on. Nor is anti-Englishness the sole criterion; nor knowledge of local people, history and scandals. All these attributes work together to make a person more or less Welsh. But although the rungs of the

Welsh ladder are not so easily discernible as those of the English ladder; and I doubt if I would have used the term ladder except for ease of comparison, the term having already been employed in describing status systems, nevertheless the rungs are there: people are thought of as being more or less Welsh, and are thought more or less highly of according to how Welsh they are.

The existence of a local prestige ladder unifies the parish of Llan. Resistance to Anglo-Americanization must take this form in many parts of the world. From the analysis of the North Welsh position made above it appears that young people growing up in societies where there are two main opposing systems of awarding prestige fall into four groups.

First there are the young people who become anglicized to be modern; to be in the swim. They feel very little conflict.

Second, there are the young people who stay at home, ignoring the new ways because they hardly notice them or because they feel they have not the confidence, adaptability or boldness to follow the new ways.

Third, there are the true resisters: the young people who stay at home, whatever their abilities, because they feel that to leave would be to betray their roots, their home, their people and the old ways they love and respect; to sell out to nondescript mass-produced manners.

Fourth, there are the regretters: the young people who have become anglicized by their parents' ambition or as a secondary unplanned effect of their own ambition to do something useful or to learn about something in which they are interested, but who feel that their anglicization is a betrayal. They try to return to their own group, but to do this is very difficult for them; and because their manners and speech mark them off from the local people, they may try some top and official link such as becoming active politically in nationalist movements. Their knowledge and understanding of their own people, their desire to be accepted by them, and the skills they have learnt at the same time as they become Anglo-Americanized, often equip members of this fourth group as political leaders. In the English class system, an equivalent to this fourth group of regretters is formed by the educated working-class youths who find they have become cut off from working-class life and wish to return.

In the English class system, early school-leavers are the equivalent to the third group, the resisters; the group who resist all pressure to climb the Anglo-American prestige ladder.

I have suggested that opposing systems of awarding prestige operate in North Wales, where I have called them the Welsh prestige ladder and the English prestige ladder. But for purposes of comparison the term Anglo-American prestige ladder is more useful, because that same 'English ladder' finds an opposing ladder in England too. It has been found that most people in England and America rate occupations according to the prestige of each, in very much the same way. This does not mean they have no other way of awarding prestige. People usually know what is wanted when they are given a questionnaire to complete. The two ladders exist side by side. A doctor is respected just because he is a doctor, in Deptford, in Llan and in Hampstead. But I think it is true to say that a warmer respect is given to a 'real local' in Llan, in the many English working-class cultures which have peculiarities of dialect, moral code and social organization, or in any community which has a living tradition. Opposing systems of awarding prestige operate in England, in Wales and in many other societies.

The two groups which understand best the existence of the two ladders and feel the attraction of both are the people described above as the third and fourth groups: the resisters and the regretters. Fear of being traitors to the home group and the attraction of the home prestige ladder account for both resistance and regrets. These forces act differently upon men and women. For a woman it is more difficult to start climbing the Anglo-American prestige ladder: she is not so often educated to do so. If she has the encouragement, the education, the capacity, or can marry 'up', she rarely resists the temptation. And once she does begin to climb to any substantial height, she rarely looks back, she rarely regrets. Men are more vulnerable to the appeal of the home ladder because it usually contains an appeal to their masculinity. They were brought up to think it is manly to do manual work; from an early age they have heard strength praised as proof of manliness. They are taught the local values in their gangs, at the same time as their sisters, perhaps, were hearing from their parents only that they should 'get on'.

I have gone beyond the scope of my study but think that the idea of opposing prestige ladders can be usefully extended beyond North Wales to other societies.

In suggesting such a comparison I should like to make a further point on the subject of prestige. It is often mentioned that people who choose to rise in the social scale in the accepted sense, that is, in my terminology, to gain marks on the Anglo-American prestige ladder, drop those of their kin who are not helpful to them in their climb. This happens naturally in Llan when, as is most common, to rise socially means to leave the district; the person in question leaves behind him spatially as well as socially those of his kin who are not go-getters. But when I found two prestige ladders operating in Llan, it reminded me of what I had observed in London as well as in Llan, that is that there were two sides to the 'dropping kin' question and that for most purposes other than that of borrowing money in a crisis, the kin of a social climber tend to drop him.

Age, whether a person works in the parish or not, and which part of the parish a person lives in, may all counteract the tendency of any individual to acquire 'English prestige'. But there are no Welsh professionals in Llan and however young a Llan person is, whichever part of the parish he lives in, however 'good' his job, modern his car, smart his clothes, and fluent his English, he feels to a greater or lesser extent the pressure of the main values current in the locality and is forced to retain some of his Welshness so long as he stays in the district.

I have taken the parish of Llan as my unit of study. Llan is divided into parts, each of which could itself have been the unit. Had I taken Carmel, Pensarn or Aber as my unit of study, I would have found even fewer social distinctions. I would have found quarrels, snobbish feelings, individuals who are looked down on or up to for the money they have or have not got, for their personal habits or their morals; but not divisions into groups, one group being above the other. Similarly, if I had taken rural North Wales as my unit of study I would have found fewer social distinctions: the towns receive the socially mobile; and those who are socially 'top' in the countryside are English.

Llan is neither the small compact community like Carmel which has no room for any divisions at all; nor the broad area which is rural North Wales, a picture of which is big enough to swallow tiny deviations and hesitant people. It contains a group of white-collared workers, most of them living in the parish's centre, Dinas. Their presence there makes Dinas less of a community than the other villages in the parish and their equivocal social position makes it untrue to say there are no social distinctions in the parish. Nevertheless they are slight and difficult for an outsider to recognize. Quarry workers and road cleaners have played and still play as prominent roles on the Parish Council and on the chapel's bench of deacons as do farmers or school teachers. The young office-workers who are becoming anglicized cannot waver for long between the two prestige ladders I have described. If they become really anglicized, it will be very hard for them to live in the parish and they probably will not want to. If the girls do not find their rich English husbands, they will have to marry manual workers and become 'Lizzie Pensarn' or 'Mati Ty-unnos'. One of the girls who belongs to this group is now in England training to be a nurse and nursing has long been a popular career for North Welsh girls. Apart from this girl, eight Llan women of the present generation have trained as nurses. Five of them worked away from home for some years and then gave up nursing to settle down in Llan. One married a local man before she had completed her training. Only two have so far stayed in England.

Neither income nor occupation serve to divide up in any clear or permanent way the Welsh people of Llan. The chapter on religion will show that the church/chapel division does no more than rally temporary groupings for specific occasions. The unity of the parish and the Welshness of its inhabitants are strengthened by the presence of representatives of the outside ruler – the English: in the persons of the landlords all the year round; and in the persons of the regular visitors, in the holidays.

As I explained in Chapter Two, feelings towards these representatives are neither unanimous nor undivided; since the representatives are individuals with whom Llan people have personal relationships. A less ambiguous antagonism is felt for England and for others of its representatives: the officials who actually administer the foreign law and send the forms in the foreign tongue; though these officials are usually Welsh. In their role as officials, at least, they are enemies.

CHAPTER FOUR

FARMING

FARMING is the most important single occupation in Llan and in this chapter I shall discuss the social position of farmers, because this relates to my discussion of social distinctions in the parish, give a brief description of the work and life on the farms and describe systems of co-operation on which farmers depend.

Farming has not been a privileged occupation in Llan, either socially or economically. The situation is changing now but the change has affected social relations very little so far. In Llan, farming has had the position of being one of several types of manual work. Most Llan men over 40 were brought up on a smallholding or farm or on leaving school went to work on the land. Farming as a way of life is familiar to most Llan people.

Men and families in Llan have gone into and out of farming as they have gone into and out of the quarries. Five of the Welshmen now farming in the parish started farming from scratch – one having previously worked as a lorry-driver; one as a quarryman and three as farm-workers. This entry into farming by manual workers was much more common before 1939.[1] The other sixteen[2] Welsh farmers in Llan are sons of farmers, and fourteen of these took over their fathers' farms;[3]

[1] This description of workers on Welsh farms confirms this: 'The Welsh labourer frequently becomes a small farmer on his own account, and sometimes even a farmer on a considerable scale . . . There is no great gulf dividing the labourer from the farmer, while misfortune and thriftlessness, or even a mere matter of preference, occasionally compels or induces the farmer to hire himself as an agricultural labourer.' *Welsh Land. The Report of the Land Inquiry Committee. Rural* (London, 1914).

[2] This makes a total of twenty-one Welshmen farming in Llan. There are three Englishmen farming in Llan and one woman in working partnership with her brother, making a total of twenty-five farmers.

[3] One of these went not into his father's but into his uncle's farm.

49

the other two came into the parish from outside and may or may not have been helped by their fathers or fathers-in-law. To read that a man took over his father's farm may be to gain the impression that there was a simple handing over of stock and authority. This is not always the case. Two of the men who took over their fathers' farms worked in various labouring jobs before taking over the farm or before working full time on it. One of these, Harry, let the tenancy of his father's farm go to a quarry-man; and bought another farm from another quarryman who himself had recently bought it. Harry, who had worked in the quarries himself for some time, borrowed the money to buy this second farm from a kinsman who had received compensation after an accident. Thus the story of how one man, Harry, began life as a farmer, involves three quarrymen acquiring farms. Two of these, and many others, have the left parish or died and are not included in the figures given above.

I have been referring to people going into farming. They also left farming, and while one man gave up the land he was farming in another district, moved to the parish and worked as a salesman, all the other men I know of in Llan who have given up farming have done so to work in the quarry, or factory or cleaning the roads.[1]

Thus over time, families have gone into farming; others have given up farming, and the same can be said of individuals in their lifetime. How has this movement into and out of farming been possible?

Firstly most farmers rent their farms, so that a man who wanted to start farming did not have to buy land or wait for his father to leave it to him.

Secondly, until the Second World War, it was general for farm-workers to be hired for half a year and to be paid half-yearly and to live in, so that although money was very scarce and wages low, it was easier for a determined man to save than it is nowadays for a weekly wage-earner to save. A man might

---

[1] Seven men, five still living in the parish and two living outside, worked farms in the parish and then gave up farming and took up other work. In addition six men who died in the last ten years were farmers in the parish and gave up farming, to finish life as employed labourers.

get £30 for half a year's work, but he could save half of it or more if he tried. He got it in a bulk sum and the chapel code caused his employer and his family to exert pressure on him to save. The farm-worker who frequently asked his employer for money, before the half-yearly pay-day had arrived, was frowned upon and there was a tendency to regard him as a waster, a rebel, a drinker. Drinking was the only entertainment available to a Llan farm-worker which had to be paid for, before the Second World War.

Thirdly, pieces of land of varying sizes could be had. Galonuchaf and Pencerrig are under twenty acres each. The combination of farms worked by the Wenallt family spreads over a total of more than 650 acres. This variety in sizes is due to changes affecting farming in the district over the past 150 years. Before the industrial revolution affected North Wales, bringing work in the quarries and on the roads, but bringing also sharply rising prices, a piece of land from twenty to forty acres could keep a man and his family, depending on the size of his family, that is, upon the size of his labour force and upon the number of mouths he had to feed. When the quarries came, prices rose but the men living on the farms were able to supplement their incomes by going to work. The factory was opened in a neighbouring parish in 1869 and provided further alternative employment. The farms of the parish became smallholdings. (My definition of a smallholding is a piece of land worked by a man who gets part of his income, most of the time, by also being employed elsewhere.) There are still five men and one woman in the parish who keep smallholdings and go out to work. In addition two men and two women own small plots of land which they let to other farmers. Before 1939, many farms in the parish were farmed by families the head of which went out to work elsewhere during the day: that is to say they were smallholdings. Since then, partly owing to the rise in the expected living standards of the people, and partly owing to the rise in the cost of living, there has been a tendency for the smallholdings to be amalgamated into large farms.

The development I have outlined in the history of Llan farms has taken place unevenly. In addition, what were first farms and later smallholdings varied in size according to the quality of their land and the size of family working them. Therefore there have been parcels of land of varying sizes coming up for rent from time to time. A man could save out of his earnings enough to buy one or two animals; move into a smallholding and, with his wife's help, run this while he continued to work elsewhere and tried to build up his stock, and so make enough money to be able to move into a larger farm.

Thus the movement into farming was possible, between the time when the quarries and factory came and the end of the war: that is roughly from 1850 to 1945. Since the war, more capital has been needed and farming has become less of a job into which any determined man could go.

Why, then, did men who had once achieved the independent status of farmer give up their farms and go to work as labourers elsewhere? Some individuals were bad managers and simply failed as farmers. This appears to have been the case with two of the farmers who turned to labouring. But why did the others give up farming and why did farmers' sons not become farmers?[1]

Mainly because economic returns were not great by comparison with wages outside except on a large, well-equipped farm, but hours were long and responsibility and risks were great. It was fairly easy to start farming a small farm, and indeed farms were often empty, the landlord unable to find a tenant. For the same reasons it was hard to make a living on such a farm.

Partly because the sale of a farm's stock in a man's late middle age meant a comfortable supplement to a regular wage in late life.

Partly because the independent status of farmer is not so valuable if the farmer is only a tenant farmer as it is if the farmer owns his own farm. Men who own a farm of a size off which they can live have a strong incentive not to give up farming, though here again, if their sons do not wish to continue, they may well sell the farm in late life.

A further reason why farming as a way of life is not clung to by families and individuals who have farmed is that in Llan, at

[1] Four farmers' sons living in the parish are non-farmers and in none of the four cases did their fathers' farms go to one of their brothers.

least, the old Welsh culture and the feeling of community is as strong amongst most other workers as amongst farmers. As I explained in the first chapter, other workers have their lives and work fused together harmoniously as much as farmers do. There is little division between living and working in the lives of most Llan people. Quarrymen, factory workers, road cleaners, farmers, farm-workers, all live and work in a community and their lives form a satisfactory whole. This is no more true of farmers than it is of everyone else and a man does not lose prestige by giving up farming.

In Llan there is no tradition that a farmer's son should marry a farmer's daughter or vice versa, whereas Rees writes that the marriage of a farmer's daughter to a labourer in Llanfihangel-yng-Ngwynfa could lead to lasting estrangement,[1] Rees's parish is near to the English border, its farms consist of better land than do the farms of Llan, and most of its farmers own their own farms. Farmers in Llan are not a distinct or superior social class. Since the war many of them have become prosperous but they do not use their growing incomes to cut themselves off from other manual workers; on the contrary they pride themselves on still going out in their old age to dig a ditch or join a shearing party. They are far more likely to vote Labour or Welsh Nationalist than to vote Conservative,[2] even when they own considerable property. English equals rich; and the Welshman who is rich cannot live as though he were, without becoming 'English'. Only eight of the twenty-two farms have bathrooms and two of

[1] A. D. Rees, *Life in a Welsh Countryside* (Cardiff 1950). In Llan out of sixteen married farmers' daughters living in the parish, ten have married manual workers and six have married farmers. Out of twenty-one Welsh farmers living in the parish, only six have married farmers' daughters. Eleven have married women who were not farmers' daughters and four are unmarried. (I do not count as farmers' offspring the children of those men who used to farm and gave it up, since I have already referred to those men's careers as evidence of the low status of farming in relation to other parts of Great Britain. Nor do I count children of smallholders.) About the whole of Wales it was written in 1894, 'The daughter of a farmer will, without losing caste, marry a labourer who hopes to become a farmer.' *Report of Royal Commission on Labour, 1891–94.*

[2] Whereas almost everyone in the Cumberland town of Gosforth votes Conservative. W. M. Williams, *Sociology of An English Village* (London 1956).

these house paying guests in the summer; five farms have no tractors.

A widespread view that the farming population in Britain is stable is often voiced in novels and plays in some such phrase as 'There's always been a Jones at Mill Farm'. Some indication how far from true this is of Llan can be gained from the list of occupants of some of Llan's farms during the past ninety years, in Appendix 2.

A force of thirty-nine men work on Llan's twenty-two farms;[1] twenty-five farmers, four farmers' sons working on their fathers' farms,[2] and ten farm-workers. Fifteen of the farms can be broadly classified as lowland farms and eight as mountain farms.[3]

The lowland farmers make most of their money either by selling milk or by rearing calves; while the mountain farmers make most of their money by selling wool and sheep. All the mountain farmers keep some cattle as well as sheep; and all the lowland farmers keep sheep either all the year round or in the winter. All farmers in Llan keep some poultry, and in some this is a major source of income.

[1] The twenty-two farms include one which comes under my definition of smallholding given above. The farmer concerned regularly supplements his income from the holding by doing odd jobs, but as he is the only small-holder with a mountain flock I have found it convenient to include his land among the farms. The twenty-two farms exclude land which is rented or owned and worked entirely by people who do not belong to the parish. I have not considered farms outside the parish owned or held by farmers living in the parish.

[2] Where a farmer's son is working in full partnership with his father or where authority has devolved from father to son but the father goes on working with his son, I count the two men as two farmers. There are two cases like this; and one farm which two brothers work in partnership and one farm which a brother and sister work in partnership; giving eight farmers for four farms. There is one farm with a bailiff and no farmer in charge and so the figures show only three more farmers than there are farms.

[3] The land of two farmers includes both types of farm. In one case I have counted the man's land as two farms. In the other case the mountain farm is outside the parish and the lowland farm is in the parish and I have only counted the lowland farm. They, like many other Llan farmers, in fact work what were, before the Second World War, a number of distinct holdings.

I shall describe the life of a mountain farmer as though he were a sheep-farmer and nothing else, and describe the life of a lowland farmer as though his only stock were cattle. No farmer in Llan is like this. My 'mountain farmer' and 'lowland farmer' are thus abstractions from reality, and this should be borne in mind especially when financial estimates are given below.

The mountain farmer's year begins with the lambing season when he patrols his flock twice a day for about a month; acting as midwife in difficult cases; trying to persuade ewes who have lost their lambs to suckle a motherless lamb or one of twin lambs; taking sheep 20 miles to the nearest vet., if necessary; and hoping, by the end of this time, to have eighty lambs:[1] approximately forty ewes and forty wethers, for each hundred of his flock of ewes. Lambing begins early in April and shortly afterwards the whole flock is sent up the mountain, the new arrivals having been ear-marked and wool-marked with the sign and mark of the farm to which they belong. Mountain farms may either have a mountain or part of a mountain, fenced off, included in their land, or rights to keep a certain number of sheep on an open mountain. There is a prohibition on putting fences round pieces of open mountain. When a number of farmers' flocks graze an open mountain, the sheep know their own part of the mountain and rear their lambs there. Because of this knowledge, called 'cynefin', these sheep have an extra value when sold to the next tenant who comes into the farm. If new sheep were bought and put on an open mountain they would have to be taught their place. The shepherd would tie a front-foot to their necks and stay up the mountain with them almost constantly until they knew their place. This 'raising the knowledge' in the sheep ('codi cynefin') was done in the past, when the mountains were understocked because of deaths in the flocks or previous poverty, and a farmer wished and was able to increase his flock quickly. Nowadays, it is generally true to say that the farmers are grazing as many sheep as they have grazing rights for; but should they wish to increase their flock they would do so by selling fewer ewes than usual. The sheep's knowledge of their part of the mountain is a

[1] Some of the hundred ewes will not conceive; some of the lambs will die; and there will be miscarriages.

substitute for boundary fences and round-the-year shepherding, and so when mountain sheep are sold it is always to an incoming tenant: they are not sold off the farm and their cynefin is sold with them. If a sheep farmer kept too many sheep on the mountain he shared with other farmers his sheep would suffer very badly before his neighbours' suffered; because of the cynefin. His sheep, although crowded and undernourished, would still keep very largely to his part of the mountain. Nevertheless, in such circumstances, there would be some spread and if the overstocking farmer were a very large farmer and his neighbour were very small, his neighbour could not stand a small loss so well as he could stand a large loss. He could 'push his neighbour over' a little, by making him reduce his flock first.

The flocks are sent up to the mountain in the spring and brought down in the winter at a time agreed upon by all the farmers concerned and fixed beforehand so that no one flock is longer on the mountain pasture than the others. During the summer the sheep are brought down to be shorn and dipped in insecticide. The new grass which grows on hayfields after the hay has been cut is called the 'aftermath' and in late summer the wether lambs are brought down from the mountain and fed either on this rich 'aftermath' or on rape specially grown for the purpose. Fattened thus for a month or two, they are then sold, together with the oldest ewes, since at lambing time the farmer's flock was nearly doubled, but his grazing remained sufficient for only the original number of sheep. The old mountain ewes are sold at the age of about five years to lowland farmers. By the time they have reached this age their teeth are worn down by years of hard grazing and their general condition is such that they can only be kept alive and lambing on richer pasture.

After the autumn sales, the flock is brought down from the mountain, the spring's lambs being wintered in the lowlands and the rest spending the winter in the fields around the farmhouse.

In 1959, a season when prices were low for the farmers, a sheep farmer in Llan got about £2 10s. for a wether lamb and £2 15s. for an ewe, in the autumn sales. The season before he had paid £1 10s. a head for wintering his lambs and his accounts, if he had a flock of four hundred sheep,[1] would look like this:

In		Out	
Sale of 160 ewes at £2 15s. each	£440	Wintering 160 ewe lambs:	£240
Sale of 160 lambs at £2 10s.	400	Rent of farm	80
Sale of wool at 4s. 6d. per lb. (2½lb. wool per sheep)	315[2]		
	£1,155		£320
		Balance or preliminary net revenue	£835

He has to keep one or two working dogs, buy dip, marking ink, shears, medicines, wire for fencing and other equipment and must have a horse or a tractor to bring his hay in. A certain number of his flock must be expected to die every year. (I mention here only the expenses and income he has in connection with the sheep he keeps. As stated above, all sheep farmers keep some cattle.) He may receive a Hill Farming Grant,[3] or a Small Farmers' Grant.[4]

[1] The average flock on mountain farms in Llan is 440, the numbers ranging from 120 to 700. By 'flock' is meant 'flock of breeding ewes'. The total number of sheep held fluctuates through the year. It always includes some rams. From April to September/October it includes the current year's wether and ewe lambs; from October it includes the current year's ewe lambs as well as the previous year's ewe lambs which will breed for the first time in the following April, when they will take the place in the flock of the 5-year-old ewes sold in October.

[2] Sale of wool from 560 sheep, i.e. 400 breeding ewes and 160 of last year's immature ewe lambs.

[3] The Hill Farming Act provides for a 50 per cent grant of the estimated cost of improvements suggested by the Hill Farm Officer, who is usually trained as an Estate Agent. It covers improvements to the farm-house and to the fields, i.e. bathrooms and electric fences; new windows and drainage of the land. It is comprehensive – the farmers must do all the improvements suggested and not just the ones he wants to do.

[4] The Small Farms Scheme is for farmers who have not got an improvement scheme going on still under the Hill Farms Grant; whose acreage

He has to know how to shear, work dogs, recognize ailments such as foot-rot, maggot, and so on, and deal with them, study market prices and build or at least mend dry-stone walls. His life is seen as picturesque and romantic by the visitors from outside and holiday makers like to watch a communal shearing or see sheep-dogs gathering the flock on the mountain. I suspect it is not only to visitors but also to the Welsh population that the sheep-farmer's life seems romantic, for although there are more lowland farms than mountain farms in the parish, the idea of a typical farmer which people have in their minds is a sheep-farmer up in the mountains. The patriarch of song and story is the sheep-farmer though, as I explained above, the sheep-farmer who lives only on sheep does not exist in Llan.

In place of the periodic, intensive work of the shepherd, the lowland farmer, living mainly by the sale of milk or the sale of cattle, has more routine daily work. He has more cows to milk and calves to feed; more buildings to clean out; more fetching and carrying; moving manure; bringing and taking cattle to and from market; taking hay and other food to his cowsheds. For him the most important time of the year is haymaking, since hay is virtually the only crop grown in Llan and is the main winter food given to cattle. Rain frequently ruins much of the crop, so that after weeks of futile work piling the cut hay into moulds to keep the worst of the rain off; then spreading the wet hay out to dry; then piling and spreading again, the farmers have to buy hay from outside the district. The practice of making silage which is gathered green, when the weather is bad, is spreading and a subsidy is paid by the Ministry of Agriculture towards the building of silos.

A lowland farmer living mainly by the sale of milk will have a yield of approximately nine and a half gallons per week per cow and one with a herd of sixteen[1] milking cattle would sell

[1] The average milking herd kept in lowland farms in Llan is a herd of sixteen; ranging from twelve to twenty-five.

---

of ploughable land is between 20 and 100 acres and whose farm work adds up to between 250 and 450 of what the Ministry of Agriculture defines as standard man days. The farmer must have a plan by which with the help of the 50 per cent grant under the scheme he can increase the productivity of his farm permanently.

£22 16s. worth of milk per week on an average throughout the year. Additional income from the sale of cattle varies with each individual farmer. Five lowland farmers sold an average of 180 dozen eggs in the year 1960 and as the average price paid them over the year for a dozen eggs was 3s. 8d. their extra gross income from egg sales averaged £34 10s.

The lowland farmer will have heavy drainage and medical expenses, as well as the major expenses of keeping milking equipment and of providing winter fodder and the usual outgoings of rent, the cost of fencing material, and a tractor.

In 1958 the Ministry of Agriculture gave the following figures for farm income for the year ending February 1958. *Welsh dairy farms based on an average size of 108 acres,* increased their revenue from £4,300 in 1956–7 to £4,553, their expenditure from £3,683 in 1956–7 to £3,766, their net income from £723 in 1956–7 to £921. It should be borne in mind that of Welsh counties, Merioneth has the lowest rent per acre for farmland (indeed the Merioneth figure is the lowest for any county in England and Wales); that is, it is one of the poorest counties, if not the poorest county, agriculturally; so that Llan figures would be lower than this.

These figures may be compared to similar figures given for *Cheshire and North Shropshire, dairy farms, based on an average size of 136 acres,* which increased their revenue from £8,520 in 1956–7 to £9,305; increased their expenditure from £7,544 in 1956–7 to £7,629 and increased their net income from £1,311 in 1956–7 to £1,789, *and S.W. Lancs. dairy farms based on an average size of 137 acres,* which increased their revenue from £9,278 in 1956–7 to £10,910; increased their expenditure from £8,499 in 1956–7 to £9,072; increased their net income from £737 in 1956–7 to £1,832.

Some of the lowland farmers live mainly not by the sale of milk but by rearing calves.

A lowland farmer may be receiving a Hill Farming Grant[1] if he does not earn his living mainly from the sale of milk; a

---

[1] The Ministry of Agriculture's definition of a 'Hill Farm' is any upland farm or farm with some of its land in the hills, whether or not it has a mountain flock, whereas I call lowland farms all those which do not have mountain flocks.

Hill Cow Grant;[1] a Small Farmers' Grant; a Calf Subsidy;[2] or a Farm Improvement Grant.[3]

He has to know how to recognize and treat ailments in his cattle and know the direction of flow of water on his apparently quite flat fields and much else about ditching and draining. He should be able to tell when the cattle are thriving, and when they are not and need, therefore, new grazing. He should know, as should his upland counterpart, the fine art of bargaining. Much time is spent on long-drawn-out negotiations. Bargaining, enjoyed as a game and believed in as an efficient method of economic success, is found in most peasant societies, but in North Wales the tempo is unusually leisurely, for Europe at least. In Italy, the seller will walk away in disgust at an offer – but walk away only two short steps and then walk back. In North Wales, he will keep away for two days (in the case of an animal); two months (in the case of land he has to rent); two years (in the case of a building); if he thinks the prospective buyer will be softened by such treatment. The pretended lack of interest, the deviousness of approach, the sophisticated and complex methods by which bargaining is pursued, are similar to the methods used in all other social intercourse in North Wales and it could be that Welsh 'not knowing' in gossip, in relations with social 'superiors', in reconciling chapel morality with real-life behaviour, is an extension of methods first used in economic exchanges.

I have outlined roughly the work on a simplified model of a sheep farm in Llan and on a simplified model of a lowland farm in Llan. In fact, each farm is unique and the work on each varies according to its size, its type of land and the personality, capability and capital of the farmer. The most striking variation

[1] A Hill Cow Grant is a payment of £10 per cow per annum paid to farmers who have regular breeding herds of beef-type cattle on their farms. Farmers under this scheme are only allowed to sell their surplus milk – the calves should get first call on the milk, and the cow on whom the grant is paid should calve once a year.

[2] A Calf Subsidy is a payment made to any type of farmer of £8 per calf of beef type.

[3] A Farm Improvement Grant is a $33\frac{1}{3}$ per cent grant towards the improvement of lowland farms. Unlike the Hill Farm Grant it does not provide for improvement to the farm-house.

noticeable between farms is the variation of tempo; some farmers working at a very high pitch most of the year round; others spreading their work over a very long day but working in a leisurely fashion, happy to stop for a talk or a cup of tea with their wives or with visitors.

It will be seen from the figures given above that Llan farmers can no longer truly describe themselves as very poor. There are still about half a dozen who, having begun farming on a small scale, are content to stand still, comparatively speaking, not wanting the bustle of a money-making life, continuing with very small flocks or herds and no machinery. But the bulk of farms are changing rapidly; the farmers investing heavily in new machinery, silos, new barns, draining, ploughing and reseeding what fields they can, fertilizing, cutting bracken and spraying to kill reeds in others; improving their stock and the capacity of their land to carry more stock. This increased activity is very expensive indeed, but Government subsidies are substantial.

The present picture contrasts very strongly with the past. As I pointed out in Chapter One, Llan farm-houses are scattered widely over the parish, its twenty-two farms, with the settlements and smallholdings which lie between them, spread over 7,790 acres of land. Some indication of how poor that land is may be gathered from the fact that in 1956 the Ministry of Agriculture classified 72 per cent of farm land in Merionethshire as rough grazing, 19 per cent as permanent pasture and only 9 per cent as arable land. The average rent of farms in Merionethshire in 1957, at 10s.[1] an acre, was lower than that in any other county in England and Wales. Rocky slopes covered with bracken – more pretty than productive – and boggy land where reeds and wild irises are as plentiful as grass, make up Llan's farm-land and the most ignorant outsider can see many indications of its poverty, and of the poverty of those who worked it in the past. Horse-drawn carts were converted to use behind tractors during and after the war and these crude vehicles, with the two shafts replaced by a drawbar, can still be seen. The old parish hearse serves as a chicken coop; a wrecked British Railways lorry houses pigs. At intervals in the mountain walls appear the ends of old iron bedsteads, complete with brass

[1] Denman and Stewart, *Farm Rents* (London 1959).

knobs, and the profusion of these bedsteads was the sight which most astonished me on my first visit to Wales. Pieces of abandoned railway lines also are used as gates.

The physical isolation of the farm-houses is counteracted by close contact between the farmers. The older farmers speak as though the days of co-operation were over. In fact every day on a farm one sees evidence of the farmer's dependence on the unpaid help of his fellow farmers. One of his sheep has been found straying in someone else's land and is brought back to him; a farmer right over the other side of the parish sends a message to say he has twin lambs and one of them will do for the ewe whose lamb miscarried; his wife is brought apples and honey; he takes his cows to another farm to be bulled. These and his return services are commonplace occurrences in the farming world generally, but the give and take of machinery is such that it could be described as 'division of capital investment'. For years almost every farmer in the parish has used the machinery at J farm to crush his oats.[1] When B farm bought a ditcher, the machine was used to dig ditches on four farms before the owner used it at all on his own farm; in two cases as part of the long-term series of gift exchanges, in the other two on a money basis.

It is necessary to go into some detail about this economic co-operation in order to discover on what basis men group together for exchange purposes. It could have been that poor farmers banded together to acquire the machinery they needed; or that there were regular partnerships of one large well-equipped and one small ill-equipped farm; or that kinship was the underlying principle of grouping.

I give below a list of major transactions in which no money passed hands: loans and labour in and out of two farms, the first a small farm, the second a large one, over a period of about a year.

[1] In this case the farmers paid 1*s*. per bag to the owner of the machine who is an Englishman living outside the parish and playing little part in the gift exchanges.

Farming

Tom's farm

Out	In
LL[1] borrowed his muckspreader[2]	
ZZ borrowed his muckspreader and kale seeder	ZZ worked for him in hay
ZZ borrowed his mowing machine	
M borrowed his kale seeder	
K borrowed his tractor and trailer	
I borrowed his plough and cattle crush	
E borrowed his disc harrow	E lent him tractor in hay
E borrowed his artificial manure spreader	E lent him circular saw bench
E borrowed his hammer mill	
E borrowed his baler	
D borrowed his baler	D lent him tractor and trailer in hay
D borrowed his kale seeder	
D borrowed his disc harrow	D lent him chain harrow
D borrowed his hammer mill	D and D's son worked in hay for him for about a fortnight.
D borrowed his artificial manure spreader	
L borrowed his tractor and trailer	L worked for him in hay on several days
B borrowed his baler	B worked for him in hay
B borrowed his cattle trailer	B lent him tractor and trailer for a week

[1] Double initials for a farmer stand for one who lives outside the parish.

[2] Owned half by Tom and half by his brother D. Tom had owned a ditcher in a previous year half and half with a farmer with whom he had no ties other than that of sharing a boundary.

63

Will's farm

Out	In
X borrowed his plough	X lent him discs
T borrowed his tractor T had some cows grazing on his land for some weeks He helped T gather the hay	T lent him rake
JJ[1] borrowed his tractor and trailer	JJ and JJ's brother cut stakes for him, with him, on JJ's land
DD borrowed his mowing machine DD borrowed his ditcher	DD sprayed his rushes with anti-rush chemical. DD lent him drill to sow grass DD towed his van to garage five miles away
S borrowed his ditcher	S lent him discs, two jacks and seed drill
Lent W his tractor and trailer for a week He worked in hay for W for several days	W lent him tractor and plough W lent him baler and tractor. He dipped his sheep at W's sheep bath
	F lent him harrow
	G helped him carry bales of hay

The most important thing to note about these lists is that the exchanges go on continuously – there is no annual reckoning – and a particular loan which has no return made for it in that year may be part repayment for a service done many years before. The loans were not made in the order I have listed them: I have put the same farmer's receipts and loans side by side, but many months often separate them. Equivalence is very rough and it is not the practice to make up the balance with cash. In one year a farmer A may lend a tractor to farmer B for two days

[1] *Vide* Note 1 on the previous page.

in the winter and borrow a tractor from B in the hay season, when it is much more valuable. A then owes B something. But if A wants to use another piece of machinery that B has, he will not hesitate to ask for it; when he gets better equipped, B will come to him for loans.

From the first list, that of Tom's farm, it will be seen that in this year, at least, he has given far more than he has taken, and whilst part of this unbalance is explained by his having old 'debts', in fact for many years past he has given more, in these major transactions, than he has taken. His farm is very well equipped with machinery and he is not very short of labour. He

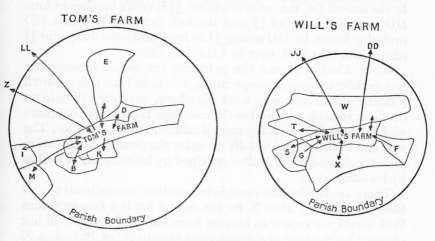

BORROWING.

does not need to borrow as much as other farmers do. He gets his return in services much smaller and vaguer than loans of machinery. His land is spread in various parts of the parish, which means that his animals are too. More than other farmers he needs his neighbours' good will in matters such as returning straying animals, or giving him or his workers a hand (perhaps for only five minutes) if they get in difficulties when *moving* animals (having a friend to block a road when a farmer is moving animals may save him hours of time), or letting him know if someone wants a cow or has a calf to sell.

The lists and the diagrams show that vicinity is a more important principle than any other. Loans from big men to small, from small to big men, from equal to equal, are all found. In theory a farmer is on borrowing terms with every other farmer he meets and if asked for the loan of something 'can't refuse'. In practice the farmers to whom a man lends are generally his neighbours in the parish. He does not lend to all those with whom he shares boundaries, however. He may not like one neighbour; another may have nothing he wishes to borrow. The principle of kinship only comes in to take the partnerships outside the parish. The farmers with whom a man is on lending terms outside the parish are usually linked to him by kinship. In the second list, that of Will's farm, JJ is Will's brother-in-law. DD is a neighbour of JJ and the link between Will and DD probably began by DD asking JJ to lend him something and JJ telling him that Will, over in Llan, had one.

While kinship is not the principle on which farmers are grouped for economic co-operation, a farm in Llan is very much a family affair. Sons may work elsewhere, but they will help on the farm at week-ends and in the evenings. Daughters sometimes wish for town life, but they can all milk and drive a tractor. The wife can milk and she usually cares for the poultry. At shearing time the sheep-farmer is always helped by his near kin as well as by his neighbours.

There are border-line cases between those a man lends to and those he hires to. Thus X on the second list is a farmer whom Will would not expect to borrow from him and whom Will has charged for the loan of machinery at various times. But when X asked him for the loan of something, Will 'couldn't refuse'. In these border-line cases, equivalence is more strict and I have heard Will say about X in another year, 'X owes me two days in the hay'.

The diagrams show the farms sharing boundaries with Will and with Tom and shows their borrowing circles. I have been describing exchanges between farmers. In the old days there were far more exchanges than there are today between farmers and non-farmers. The quarrymen and their wives would help the farmers in the hay and throughout the year the farmers would give buttermilk and potatoes to those who had helped them. Left over from these days is the practice farmers still have of giving potatoes to non-farmers each season when they dig them up. In some cases, the recipients of the potatoes have helped to sow the potatoes, but more often they have not.

Each farmer, then, has a borrowing circle, and the main principle on which it is based is neighbourliness. When the borrowing circle crosses the parish boundaries and jumps over intervening farms, it is more often than not kinship which has provided the link between the Llan farm and the distant farm.

In addition to his borrowing circle, each sheep-farmer has a shearing circle. The shearing circles are more fixed than the borrowing circles, less affected by likes and dislikes and more

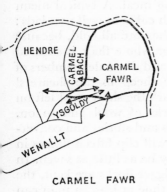
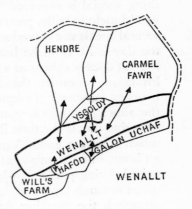

SHEARING.

definitely circles of neighbouring farms than are the borrowing circles. They cross the boundaries of the parish more because the boundary often runs across the tops of mountains on which sheep-farmers share grazing rights. The very landmark which serves to separate Llan from other parishes brings the sheep-farmers on either side of the boundary together, whereas the landmarks which help form the boundary elsewhere, ridges and rivers and bare places, tend to keep the lowland farms rather separated from other lowland farms in neighbouring parishes.

When a man takes over a mountain farm, he takes over the sheep with their knowledge of their place on the open mountain, and he takes over the shearing circle. He asks his neighbours 'Who do I shear with?' and acts according to their answer.

Ceunant has always gone to Ty Isaf shearings and so the new tenant of Ceunant goes to Ty Isaf shearings, however well or badly he gets on with Ty Isaf people.

In July the sheep are ready for shearing: a new fleece is growing and between it and the old fleece is a division: a section of weak wool. The sheep are put in an enclosure but there is not enough pasture for them to remain there long and generally the whole flock is sheared in a day. Word is sent round that Pwll-Du farm is shearing tomorrow and the traditional group, plus some kinsmen who may have travelled far, arrive for a hard day's work. The farmer's wife has helpers in the kitchen and something special is expected for a shearing meal. A typical menu would include trifle, pastries and Welsh cakes as well as salads: several meals are served and usually they are all cold, because the day is likely to be hot. The farmer whose flock is sheared himself does not shear as a rule, but he and the male members of his family organize things, carry the sheep to the shearers' benches, ear-mark the lambs, dose, mark the short wool left on the shorn sheep, carry away the sacks of wool and so on. Shearing day is the time for arguments and stories and conversation is always good. A good shearer will clip fifteen fleeces in an hour, but a man's contribution may be as little as seven. In neighbouring parishes, where much bigger flocks are kept, the speed is much higher and, for a short time at least, a man can approach the shearing machines which clip twenty an hour. Shearing time for some farmers is also haymaking time and the days spent in visiting neighbouring farms to shear are hard spared. In the past, flocks were small and there were more men on the land. Mechanization and emigration have left 1·8 men per farm on Llan's land. None of Llan's mountain farmers have used machines to shear, but when they do the bonds that tie the farming community together will have been weakened by one strand.

CHAPTER FIVE

PARTISANS IN PEACETIME

THERE is a lot of water in the mountain streams around Llan parish in November and the salmon jump up the waterfalls to spawn. No one goes on aimless strolls – they go to the bridge to see if the water is high and, finding it is, they go home to sort out gaffs, nets, hooks, torches and voluminous coats that will hide this poaching gear. Some prefer to use a large home-made net of wire, providing the water is not running so fast as to wrench it from them; some prefer to spear or spike the salmon as they swim past; some just use their hands and catch the fish when they are lying still and they say the salmon like being stroked at spawning time. Some prefer the daytime when they can see the bailiffs coming; some prefer the night when it is easy to hide and the bailiffs might be in the pub. But whatever the time, whatever the means, anyone who is Welsh[1] goes poaching. When I say anyone, I mean men only, of course.

During the poaching season, wives are neglected, not for money-consuming beer, but for supper-helping salmon and they would rather their men came in excited from an evening's sport than lethargic or quarrelsome from an evening's drinking. This is one reason why, although it is the women whose tongues seize most sharply on any breach of the chapel code and who feel genuine shock and fear evil consequences if hay is carried on a Sunday, the women condone their husbands' 'criminality'. The other more important reason is that they do not consider poaching to be wrong.

What are the men's motives? The fish are eaten and relieve the monotony of the Welsh diet, but fresh salmon, fried, steamed, grilled and baked, itself gets monotonous very quickly

[1] As explained in Chapter Three, men climbing the English prestige ladder do not go poaching.

over the five or six weeks of the poaching season. Further, the
quality of the fish is believed to deteriorate after the first couple
of weeks – larger fish come up the streams and those which have
spawned and are returning to the sea have flabby flesh. On the
whole the poachers are not very keen on eating the fish: they
cannot sell them to hotels or fishmongers because salmon are out
of season. So a large proportion of the fish a man catches, he
gives away, perhaps to his foreman, perhaps to the minister,
perhaps to relatives or friends living outside the district. To
give gifts in this way is to store up credit of some kind, but there
is a great deal of barter and gift exchange taking place all the
time. So many other objects and services are used in these exchanges that I do not think that the hope of receiving a return is
a major motive causing the men to catch salmon. The economic
incentive is not a sufficient one in these days, though it seems to
have been more important in the past, when, it is said, a much
larger proportion of the fish caught was eaten in the parish.

A further attraction might seem to be the danger. But in fact
the danger hardly exists: poachers are very rarely caught. The
comparative safety of poaching in the area follows from the fact
that river bailiffs, like other officials, are either with the poachers
or against them. A bailiff who is part of the community wants to
drink and play darts with the men he is supposed to hunt; he
and his family depend on the co-operation of their neighbours
and their life would be impossible if he did his job well. Any
river bailiff who is not part of the Welsh community has a
rather dangerous job, especially when he is working away from
home. Poachers will not hesitate to gang up on him or take him
on singly if he traps them or catches them after a chase. A few
years ago a murderously sharp hook narrowly missed the head
of one bailiff. In the old days bailiffs were stoned and thrown in
the river and old men still carry stones in their pockets when
they go to the river. Such bitter warfare is rarely waged nowadays. But dating back as far as the tradition that small farmers,
farm-workers and quarrymen in this poor district win few battles
in the class war, is the tradition that they usually win this kind
of battle. There is another weapon which has grown in use as
violence has lessened and this weapon provides another reason
why poaching in Llan and the district is not dangerous and also

demonstrates an interesting aspect of the social structure of rural North Wales. This weapon is what has been called in other environments the grapevine. The movements of the river bailiffs, as of other officials, are known within at least a ten-mile radius from their base. Adults and children have an amazing capacity to remember registration numbers of cars and motor-cycles and they notice number, colour and make so casually and invariably that the mobile maps they carry with them seem to occupy a dimension of their minds which I lack. London schoolboys collect car numbers, but it is quite a different phenomenon I am discussing. I have heard a woman of over 50 who has always lived in isolated farmsteads and who can speak no English, mentioning car numbers as often as people's names in her conversation. Girls of 7, teenagers, village housewives, all know the numbers or at least can recognize at a glance, the important cars of the district, as well as the most familiar ones. For the most important cars are not seen every day, but when seen they are noticed. Everyone you meet stops for a brief talk and mentions:

'The Pentre police car passed down towards Hafoty just now.'

'Are you sure? There's a court case on in town this morning.'

'Well, it's XXX33, isn't it?'

Or: 'Jack saw Twm Bailiff going up by Wern at dinner-time. At least it was his motor-bike. That red Excelsior ZZZ11.'

Young men from this district, when on a spree in London, feel nostalgia when they see a car with a home registration number. And many can recognize some particular cars and motor-bikes by their sound. Knowing vehicles is not a hobby, it is part of the business of living, generally because communications are of great importance, and particularly because the grapevine is a war weapon.

After a court case which followed a skirmish between poachers and bailiffs in 1959, the *Daily Mail* wrote about the bailiffs: 'They always talk in secret code, for they believe the poachers may have a phone-tapping source.' (3rd November, 1959). I do not think the poachers are as well or as formally organized as the bailiffs implied but the report is a tribute to the efficiency of the poachers' informal warning system.

Thus the forces of officialdom, and especially the men on the law-and-order side of officialdom, are kept constantly under surveillance, although the local population is hardly aware of the watch it keeps. The North Welsh also keep a curious eye on one another's activities, as do all country people, but one of the purposes most useful to themselves for which they employ their powers of observation and memory is to beat the officials. I shall not go into all the forms the anti-official war takes. Poaching is interesting for two reasons. Firstly, because on the face of it, it is so unimportant economically. And secondly, because unanimity is more easily reached against river bailiffs than against other officials. In a general way everyone is against the police, but just occasionally a farmer loses some sheep and in an effort to clear up the suspicions and fears that begin, in the hope of proving that it is a certain dog, or is not a certain dog, or in the hope of catching the culprit, some people will co-operate with the police. In a general way everybody is out to 'fiddle' from other officials, but most of these other officials are sometimes useful. No one at any time is on the side of the river bailiffs – in their role of river bailiff. People may think, in theory, and even go so far as to say, that it is a pity to catch salmon while they are breeding and thus diminish the supply, but in practice they go poaching. Being Welsh is more important than saving salmon. The fact that the work of the river bailiffs is seen as simply the preservation of game fish for the pleasure of rich English people, and not at all for the advantage of the local working population, makes it possible for people to unite against them and this makes poaching particularly suitable as an activity which unites people as Welsh; unites them against these representatives of English rule; unites them in an anti-official war.

It is easy to understand country people trying to avoid paying taxes. It is not so obvious why they catch fish they do not eat and go to very great trouble to do so. But here almost anything banned is worth doing, to keep the war going. I suspect that if it were forbidden by the Government to grow asparagus, and the chapel were fairly indifferent to the ban, North Welsh people would grow it although few have even heard of, never mind tasted, asparagus; few know it is thought of as a luxury food and probably no one would like it. They poach partly so that they and their friends can eat salmon, partly because poaching is a sport, partly because their fathers did it when poaching provided a vital addition to the family diet, but also largely because it is forbidden by those they see as the enemy.[1] They do not phrase all these motives in the way I have done, but it is clear from the way they speak that all these motives operate. They do not speak of a war but they speak and act as though they were engaged in one. When two boys in their teens were stopped on the road by the bailiffs and found to be carrying salmon, the feeling was widely expressed that the bailiffs were cowardly to go after such young boys and to catch them away from the river, and by a mean trick. (A bailiff had told one of the boys he would not be in Llan that night, assumed the boy would believe him, and stopped him late at night near his home.) 'We'll have to do something about those bailiffs,' the men said. Next night the air was let out of the tyres of the bailiffs' van and water put in the petrol tank.

Although salmon poaching appears to be unimportant from an economic point of view, and it is certainly so in the short run, in the long run it fulfils a function which is essential to the economic life of North Wales. For what the whole poaching conspiracy does is to draw the people of North Wales very close together. There is very little class feeling inside the structure of North Wales society, as I have explained in an earlier chapter. The upper class, the owners of quarries and land, as well as the foremen in any large enterprise, have been traditionally English; power and money and property in Wales have long been in the hands of Englishmen or anglicized Welshmen – so much so that there is still a general tendency to classify all English visitors as upper class. The bloody Saxons – minus a man's particular English friends – are excluded from conversation by an insistence on the use of the Welsh language; milked for drinks in the pubs; and foiled when they appear as officials.

[1] I had the impression that the number of conscientious objectors in Llan from 1939 to 1945 was higher than average but had not the time to compile the figures needed to test this impression, i.e. number of men liable for call-up in the population as it existed then and the proportion who did not serve because of exemption and because of conscientious objection.

Hostility is extended to those Welshmen who do 'their' jobs, or adopt 'their' ways. Class antagonism is expressed through and disguised as nationalism. The anti-English feeling (which is not so much violent as all-pervading) is expressed by a group which extends far beyond the minority who vote Welsh Nationalist. It is the form which class conflict takes, and the disguise in which many social antagonisms appear. English people known to be definitely not mean, rich or snobbish, are warmly accepted into the community, although if they have jobs as officials they will be treated in one way as men and in quite another way as officials. In Chapter Two I distinguish between two levels of anti-English feeling; that mixed feeling which is directed towards individuals; and the 'partisan' feeling which is directed towards the abstract idea of 'ruling England'.

Country people's resentment of town bureaucracy is a world-wide phenomenon. In North Wales, this antagonism, like most other social hostilities, is expressed in nationalistic terms.

Officialdom is seen as an English phenomenon, a concrete expression of English power, which can be recognized and resisted; and the war against it, as in the case of the poaching grapevine, cuts across village quarrels, differences in income, religion, age and sex and draws all these Welsh-speaking people together. Any mechanism which helps to do this is clearly important economically, since co-operation is a must in this poor country of scattered farmsteads, where all machinery and skilled labour is shared among the farmers and all private transport (except that of officials and 'big people') is shared by everyone.

The poaching conspiracy has a significance greater than the personal motives avowed by those engaged in it. It is an annual event which strengthens ties between the inhabitants of the district. To engage in it is a sign of Welshness. It symbolizes the fellowship of people who are physically separated from one another in scattered dwellings, who have many causes to quarrel, but who need one another all the year round, and who show they are 'on the same side' every November.

As I said in the preface, I do not believe it is the work of the social anthropologist to relate people's activities to their motives. It has been suggested to me that if I say the poaching conspiracy creates solidarity among the North Welsh people then I must go further and either say that the North Welshman goes poaching with the conscious aim of creating solidarity or I must suppose that he has an unconscious desire for solidarity.

I think that a person's motives for doing most things are mixed and not easily recognized and distinguished one from the other, by himself or by outsiders, and I do not think the social anthropologist is required to try to do this sorting out. There is no reason to suppose any poacher has a conscious or unconscious desire for solidarity. Last season or the season before, though he went poaching for various reasons which may have differed from those of his colleagues, he may have shared with them a satisfactory feeling of comradeship which followed the poaching. Enemies may have forgotten quarrels and run to give him a warning, and he may then have felt that this meant he could not continue the quarrel. Nevertheless this comradeship of last season may well be forgotten when he goes poaching. He may have fresh in his mind some nuisance a neighbour has committed rather than a feeling of brotherhood with him. But the feeling of brotherhood will again follow from participation in the poaching season. In his mind he does not relate warning Sam that there is a car on the bridge with the fact that he might one day need to borrow Sam's van.

Solidarity is an outcome of the activity. In the same way, other minor satisfactions may follow on a man's participation in a poaching season. He may see a heron fishing, or a badger playing and find pleasure in it. He would not go out the next year with the intention or hope of seeing such things but they may be some of the pleasant associations with the idea of poaching which help to make it attractive to him. This would be one of the many motives a psychologist might find in some particular poacher's mind. To find it and to estimate its degree of consciousness is not for the anthropologist, who is studying a social situation and the effects on a group of its own and other groups' behaviour.

Poachers do not all have the same motives and often they may go simply because they want a fish. However, they frequently catch more than they know what to do with. My suggested explanation may stand or fall, but it does not stand or

75

fall by my finding or failing to find satisfactory psychological links.

The chapel brought people together in the past and was the central symbol of Welshness, certainly in many parts of Wales, and, I believe, in Llan; the church being the centre for English people and those who wished for anglicization. In Llan, at least, this is no longer the case. Attendances at church and chapel are small now and although church and chapel are rallying points for opposing cliques for some purposes, members of church and chapel alike are Welsh-speaking, are 'workers' and go poaching.

At present, participation in the poaching conspiracy particularly, and in the anti-English feeling generally, is a much more important and general badge of Welshness in North Wales than is the chapel. A group of people of many conflicting interests are fused together in opposition to another group, seen as outside. The motives in the people's minds as they engage in the action which brings them together are non-economic. The result of their fusion, however, is that their mutual co-operation in economic affairs is helped and I do not think the poaching conspiracy would continue in its present strength if those involved in it needed each other's support and services less.

CHAPTER SIX

IF NOT THAT LAW, WHICH LAW?

SINCE the North Welsh dislike British bureaucracy, have they a substitute for it? To what extent do the native institutions for providing medicine, education, insurance and law still survive?

The new medicine has been the service most thoroughly welcome. There was a case in Aberystwyth Court in 1957 where a man's excuse for not appearing in court was that he had to see a farmer's wife for treatment of yellow jaundice. Her diagnosis was made first by her, and then by the patient himself, measuring his forearm with a specially prepared length of wool. The test was positive and the cure depended on him wearing a length of wool round his left wrist for a certain period of time and drinking liberal doses of brandy and saffron. However, this application of an old Welsh remedy does not seem to be typical. Though I have often been told by Llan men that wearing wellington boots is bad for the eyes, a woman of 40 can remember seeing jars of leeches in a local chemist's shop, and Llan women say they 'don't believe in crawling for babies', in fact doctors, hospitals and clinics provided under the National Health Service are used by all.

In education, the native system of formal teaching survives in a weakened form. The days of eloquent fiery sermons and spontaneous prayer meetings are over, but chapel Sunday schools, which together with church Sunday schools taught many to read and write in the last century, still do much for adult education, side by side with the W.E.A. Farmers and quarrymen attend the chapel Sunday school in the nearby quarry town and use the Bible very much as a thread on which to base their discussions of philosophical, social, historical and political subjects. Quarrymen in many quarries hold formal discussions at lunch-time, with a chairman to keep order.

These discussions are not organized by the Union, or the management, but are simply traditional.

Eisteddfodau, annual Singing Festivals organized for the district by the chapels, and 'little concerts' organized by enthusiasts in the parish, are always well attended and most adults and children in Llan have sung or recited at one or many of these functions. Children from the age of four upwards go on to the platform alone and perform to a crowded hall.

These activities train people in ability to use the Welsh language well, to speak in public and to listen critically, and on formal occasions very many of them do these things in a way which contrasts markedly with their behaviour at other times. The annual book of the National Eisteddfod is widely read, copies are lent from house to house, and men will ask each other for it in the pub. This book contains the criticisms which the panels of judges made of the performances at the National Eisteddfod; it contains the plays, stories and poems submitted to the Eisteddfod and the criticisms of these. These entries and commentaries are carefully read and discussed. A farmer's wife of 30 reports to her 70-year-old father-in-law the arguments she heard at the W.E.A. meeting and learns from his comments. At one 'little concert' in Llan, one of the competitions for adults and children was a test on the tonic sol-fa scale and there was no shortage of entrants.

In Dinas school the children are trained for such occasions, can sing solo, in chorus and in parts and recite stories and poems, so that the official education system supports the native system of formal education here. In the past, when State schools discouraged the use of the Welsh language, there was a conflict between the two. What conflicts with State education now is the informal Welsh system of education; the education in 'Welshness' rather than in Welsh which children learn at home, at chapel, and at work. Official formal education in North Wales seems to be of a high standard; comprehensive schools have been functioning in the county since 1953 and the special G.C.E. exams take into account the fact that the children are Welsh-speaking. Nevertheless, there are still strong incentives for the bright child not to climb the educational ladder. To climb it means to step out of the rural world which still has a culture worth belonging to and which I have tried to describe in the introduction when I discuss the meaning of the word 'Welshness'.

I am not suggesting there are many more 'early leavers' in North Wales than elsewhere.[1] Other writers will explain the home pull which helps to account for early leavers elsewhere; I wish to try to describe that which operates in Llan.

It is easy to see in Llan the pull exerted on a bright boy by the local culture, by the Welsh value system. The pull is not against learning, which is much respected. It is not particularly against the Englishness of that learning, although more marks are given on the main prestige ladder for knowledge of 'Welsh' things – knowledge of the community and its members' histories, knowledge of Welsh songs and poems, knowledge of country skills, than for knowledge of world geography and other school subjects. The pull is mainly against the desertion of the district or, at least, of the most important group in it, which the bright child would have to make if he were to take advantage of the official educational opportunities available to him.

I have tried to describe in Chapter One and in this work generally the life which pulls at the bright adolescent and makes him an 'early leaver'. Other working-class cultures totally different in flavour and composition, but with pulls just as powerful, send the dockland boys in London and Liverpool out to work at 15, and give us witty Cockneys, bright porters and stupid students. It must be trying for university staffs to support the latter, but the former should not be considered as a loss to the country, but an investment against the time when leisure is as plentiful as hard work is now, when any working-class subcultures which survive will have a very important role to play.

The old institutions which existed before the British Civil Service came to operate effectively in North Wales still carry on in varying strengths. The new Ministry of Health is welcomed; the Ministry of Education works against a strong current of opposition from the traditional culture; and for social insurance, the family still travel far to take care of sick members, and visitors to the house where there has been a death still leave a packet of tea, some butter or money, or give money to the

[1] For figures see Appendix 3.

children of the house. Few farmers can afford to employ labour all the year round but at times of the year they all need some extra help and then unemployed men, people on holiday, perhaps a man on leave from the Merchant Navy, another farmer not very busy at the time, or a casual farm-worker, will work by contract, bargaining for a price to dig so many ditches, or cut the bracken on a certain field. If these workers know someone with a large family, or who is sick, or who has been out of work for a long time, they will invite him to share the job with them.

Help from the Government still seems rather arbitrary; welcome but not to be relied upon. Who can understand the rules and regulations by which one qualifies? British bureaucracy is an extra to existing institutions rather than a replacement of them.

I shall now go on to consider the place of law, since it is the 'law-and-order' officials who are most resented and opposed.

As I mentioned in the last chapter, it is not only by poaching that Llan people oppose officials. There was Will Felin Bach who, having hid in the mountains whenever a car approached his farm, was finally caught by the tax-collectors. They suggested that, if he did not pay tax, they could confiscate his tractor, his car, his plough. Will wished them luck and pointed out that all he owned in the way of farm machinery was a wheelbarrow. There was Twm Dinas Fawr, part-time postman in a neighbouring parish, whose round includes all the outlying mountain farms. An official came to test the length of the round with the intention of reducing the time allowed, and therefore the pay. Twm did not usually deliver letters with 1½d. stamps on until he had a real, that is to say, a personal letter to deliver. So on many days he did not have to visit every farm. On the occasion of the time test, however, with the help of the postmaster, he had saved up plenty of official letters, circulars, advertisements and added these to the real letters so that he had something for every farm on his round. 'Of course, to get from Ty Goch to Cwm you just have to cut across the black field, step across the deep ditch in that narrow place and you are practically there. But I took him halfway up the mountain wall, over the bridge and down again. And so with every farm. I rushed him up and down the mountainside until he was panting like a train. No talk after that of my taking too long to deliver the post. They gave me an extra half-hour.'

But if Llan people see policemen, tax-collectors and river bailiffs as minions of a foreign ruler, what is their attitude to the benefits which come to them through officials? And secondly, what means of their own have they of settling disputes that inevitably arise between them and to what extent do they use the foreign law?

I shall try to answer these questions in this chapter.

Very understandably the farmers accept subsidies for land improvement, drainage, rearing calves, and so on, just as they accept the accompanying price control. Both shades of government have found that a completely free market makes for uneconomical farming in the long run, with farmers switching from pigs to hens, and then to dairy stock, as prices rise and fall. Who would use milking cows to rear calves when a good price can be had for milk today? Fluctuations in price particularly effect the small farmers with little capital who live in poor districts. Small farmers lose too much in the short run when they invest for the long run. The continued existence of many of the wartime price controls and subsidy regulations acts in North Wales to stabilize the farming effort. Elsewhere it may act in another way. Here, the concentration of markets and increased competition from abroad, particularly from Australian and New Zealand sheep, create conditions under which Welsh mountain farms would not exist for long without subsidies.

Just as Welsh farmers see the reason for the subsidies, so the farm-labourers and quarrymen accept unemployment and sickness benefit and National Assistance. Are they biting the hand that feeds them when they work against other branches of the same Civil Service? Are their actions irrational? I am aware that attitudes similar to the ones I am discussing exist elsewhere than in Welsh-speaking North Wales, but I wish to talk particularly of that area and of the particular combinations of attitudes found there. For the fact that the recent history of officialdom in North Wales is different from its history elsewhere has resulted in the present situation being different from the situation elsewhere in important respects.

In 1896 the report of the Royal Commision on land in Wales and Monmouth included the statement: 'We have no doubt that in the past and occasionally at the present time, the statutes as to offences connected with game have fallen with undue severity and been applied with considerable harshness and have in many places been the source of much suspicion and unhappiness.' The report refers to 'damage to crops due to violent actions of gamekeepers or careless and discourteous exercise of sporting rights by sporting gentlemen'.

In 1955 a local magistrate said, 'In olden days when landlords and the wealthy reserved fishing rights for themselves, the public had a certain sympathy with the poacher who snatched an occasional salmon which was intended for the rich man's table.'

The suffering caused by the means test during the inter-war years of depression is well known.

Before the 1939–45 war, officials meant trouble for working-class people – they were far more often involved in stopping money, or limiting money or taking money than in giving it; they were the interferers, the arresters, rather than the people whose jobs were to distribute benefits and to judge cases fairly.

All these troubles were aggravated in the district under discussion. North Wales is one of the poorest districts of the British Isles. During depressions, suffering was great – things went from very poor to bad. The industrial areas were more vocal; the coal miners and factory workers fought. The people of North Wales were cut off from the movement and the fighting. Wirelesses and English newspapers were not common then and workers do not and did not work together in large numbers under one roof. But the people were not 'lumpen'. They saw their troubles in terms of foreign oppression rather than class war, as do all colonial people. Further, although Wales was conquered by England centuries ago the conquest was not made effective in the lives of most people in North Wales until the officials of this century brought a realization of it into their homes.

Another result of the 'colonial' situation is that Welsh ministers, teachers and doctors either associated themselves with their poorer countrymen, in which case they did not try to interpret the role of the Civil Service so much as to share the generally hostile attitude towards it; or they were thought of as English in all important respects and therefore disregarded. So that as the personnel and functions of the Civil Service changed, there was no section of North Welsh Society to identify itself with the changes and speak for the officials.

But perhaps the main cause for the special hostility which arose in pre-war days towards officials in North Wales was the language difference. Until local education authorities were founded in 1902, the Welsh language was taught in very few Welsh schools and until 1888 the use of the Welsh language was banned in the majority, so that children were taught in a language which they could not understand and were punished for speaking in the only tongue they knew.[1] Until the 1939–45 war, Welsh-speaking people were met by English-speaking officials, received letters and forms in English which they often could not understand and could less often reply to in English.

[1] This 'ban', to which so many Welsh writers refer, was not a law or regulation against the use of Welsh passed by the English Government, though very many Welsh people believe that to be the case. It was a ban imposed by heads of private and charity schools and later by Boards of Education in Board Schools; though Government policy was largely instrumental in creating it. From 1862 until 1888 Government grants were paid to schools on the basis of the attendance of the children and the results they achieved in an examination on arithmetic, reading and writing – in English. This system discouraged teachers from teaching anything but those three subjects – time spent on teaching Welsh could mean a financial loss to the school; and it was not widely thought at that time that the English language could be taught by using Welsh as the medium of instruction. But even before this system was introduced, teaching in Welsh was practised in hardly any of the schools existing in Wales, and the use of the 'Welsh not' – a board hung around the neck of the child last heard speaking Welsh – was reported some years before 1862. The early schools were financed by charities and by English or anglicized gentry and they were usually founded with the intention of teaching Welsh children the English language. For a long time the Welsh reformers who wished Welsh to be introduced into the schools argued that the main reason for doing so was that it would be the best medium in which to teach the English language.

For further information on this see 'The Place of Welsh and English in the Schools of Wales'. Central Advisory Council for Education (Wales) Report. And Welsh Department, Ministry of Education's pamphlet, No. 2, on Education in Wales, 1847–1947.

As I have explained in Chapter Three the language barrier arises in very many of the important situations of a person's life and the result of a person being obliged to use a tongue with which he is not familiar is that he feels inferior to those speaking or those writing to him. It is no more wise to humiliate people than it is to use force upon them. This English humiliation of Welsh-speaking people, however unintentional, is real, and it has created what I have described as 'partisan warfare', far more than has the historical fact that England physically conquered Wales. Awareness and resentment of England's physical conquering of Wales is often a major motive for white-collared workers to join the Welsh Nationalist Party. The fact that English is the official, legal language in Wales has turned ordinary Labour-voting, Welsh-speaking people against England and the officials who represent her.

The strong feeling of suspicion of officials, which was widespread throughout Britain in pre-war days, remains. Social injustice is not forgotten easily. There are still officials who act towards uneducated people more like their employers than their employees. In 1961 I heard an Assistance Board official say, when giving a grant to a temporarily destitute family: 'I am doing this as a favour, mind.' So that although the whole character of administration and officialdom has altered and the incidence of welcome visits has probably come to exceed the incidence of unwelcome visits, working people's hostility towards officials is changing more slowly. This is true of industrial Britain[1] and is much more true of rural North Wales. Now most officials who visit people's homes can speak Welsh and many forms which Welsh-speaking people have to complete have room for answers in Welsh, but many do not. Matrons in hospitals,

---

[1] Richard Hoggart writes that working-class people in North English towns divide the world into 'Them' and 'Us'. '"They" are "the people at the top", "the higher-ups", the people who give you your dole, call you up, tell you to go to war, fine you, made you split the family in the thirties to avoid a reduction in the Means Test allowance, "get yer in the end", "aren't really to be trusted", "talk posh", "are all twisters really", "never tell yer owt" (e.g. about a relative in hospital), "clap yer in clink", "will do y' down if they can", "summons yer", "are all in a click [clique] together", "treat y' like muck".' R. Hoggart, *The Uses of Literacy* (London 1957).

headmasters at secondary schools, magistrates in court, tend to be English. There is still a language problem and a colonial feeling. Perhaps this helps to explain the attitude of North Welsh people to the benefits which come to them through officials. People who understand the politics of the Civil Service and the complications of Government better than the rest, still cheat officials because it is against the moral code of the community not to do so.

The following story may illustrate the way in which Llan people think of their community in physical terms as though it were poised facing the officials: the actual parish looking towards the quarter from whence officials come. The road going south out of the parish leads to Salem, the factory village, where reside the nearest policeman and taxation officials with jurisdiction over Llan people's lives. The road going north out of the parish leads to a town outside the county of Merioneth: a direction from which Llan people therefore expect no threat. A wandering juvenile delinquent, originally from Birmingham, immediately an escapee from a Borstal, found his way to Llan some years ago and stole from a house there. A Llan man, discussing his movements prior to the robbery, said he had seen the boy going first towards the south to the cross-roads, and then back again, and he had obviously been going to see that the Salem road was clear of police. It could not occur to him or to his listeners that the Birmingham boy did not know from which direction police might come. For them, to see Llan with one's eyes; to see its marshes and mountains, is inseparable from seeing Llan as a group of people with their eyes on the source of officials: Salem in the south.

What means of their own have Llan people of settling disputes that inevitably arise between them?

There are three main factors which determine the action taken over the various types of offence that occur and they are:

1. The cold war against the English and officials;
2. The fact that everybody knows everybody and what they do;
3. The fact that, sooner or later, for one purpose or another, each person in the parish will be allied with each other,

though in other circumstances, or for other purposes, they
may be opposed to each other. (Evans-Pritchard, Gluck-
man, Fortes, Barnes and Frankenberg have all made this
point about other communities.)

Very few people in Llan have been taken to court for stealing,
but this does not mean there is no stealing. Of the North Welsh
who steal, the largest number do so from large, impersonal con-
cerns and official bodies; a smaller number steal from the
English landowners, and still fewer from tourists.

In these cases of thefts from outsiders, factor 1 operates. Since
everyone unites, across all barriers, in a Welsh-speaking conspiracy and the police get almost no co-operation, these cases of
theft, which are not considered immoral (stealing from impersonal bodies being considered least immoral), rarely reach
court.

There is the occasional kleptomaniac who steals from his or her
neighbours. There is one such family living in Llan, the Griffith
family, and while its members are regarded as wicked to steal
from their neighbours, and have been caught in the act of
stealing several times, the treatment is not to take them to court,
but to ostracize them as much as possible. Here factor 3
operates. The Griffith family is not taken to court because the
other children in their neighbourhood have so few playmates
that they want to play with the thieves' children although they
do not invite them to their houses because they, too, steal.
Because a nearby farmer provides milk to the family and he
wants their custom. Because, although the women who are her
neighbours rarely speak to Mrs. Griffith, if they see her in town
they feel, 'Well, at least Polly Griffith is from our row of houses
and we know her and *she* can't put on airs.' Factor 2 operates
here, too. Everyone knows everyone and everything about them.
And so Mrs. Griffith knows all the things that everyone else has
done which, if not immoral, are certainly illegal.

So if a person steals from his neighbours instead of from those
considered to be rich, it is not permissible for them to inform
the police about him; indeed they will meet with disapproval if
they inform the police about anything, whatever their neighbour does. Disputes over garden boundaries, the occasional
assault or fight, are usually coped with by informal means

without the police being called in, and most court cases of this kind involve foreigners.

So far I have discussed stealing, which tends not to reach court in Llan. But Llan people do sometimes take each other to court, although in most cases they try not to, and the cases most likely to arise in court between ordinary people (as opposed to cases which are 'people versus officials') are affiliation cases. Although the chapel is still a power in the land, the rate of illegitimacy is high and I discuss this in Chapter Eight. The bulk of affiliation cases, like most other disputes between Llan people, are settled out of court, by marriage. The average age of marriage in Llan is higher than it is in England and Wales as a whole. The reasons for this are discussed in Chapter Eight and, as pointed out there, very many marriages in Llan have taken place because the girl was pregnant. Nevertheless, five women in the parish have taken men to court alleging that they were the fathers of their children, and a man in the parish has been taken to court by a girl in a neighbouring village on the same issue. In two cases, the man had fathered children by two girls and could not easily marry both. In other cases, the men were prepared to go to court rather than marry the girl concerned for a variety of reasons.

Firstly, the circles in which young men and young women have to co-operate are very few. There is a separation between the sexes in Llan, though it is not nearly so clear-cut as that which Frankenberg found in his border village. It is, therefore, not such a serious matter for young women to take young men to court as it would be for, say, their neighbours to take Mr. or Mrs. Griffith to court. Then, where the woman concerned had a reputation as a 'good thing', a man would feel embarrassment amongst his fellows at marrying her. Factor 2 comes in here. No one can have loose sexual morals without the fact being well known, though people will pretend they do not know when talking to the person in question, and in Llan, as elsewhere, more tolerance is extended to a man in these matters than to a woman.

The important, typical disputes that arise between farmers concern sheep straying, the worrying of sheep by dogs and sheep being stolen. Cattle are not kept in unenclosed fields as are sheep, but on relatively flat land near the farm-house; they are usually seen every day; and the main herds of cattle belong to lowland farms, which are of smaller acreage, and therefore more easily supervised, than the mountain sheep-farms. For these reasons cattle do not stray so much and are not stolen or worried so easily as are sheep.

Sheep-farming is the typical, traditional farming of the mountain districts in North Wales and sheep are the most sacred form of property. Every farmer knows some of his sheep individually. In the old days sheep-stealing was considered a terrible crime and the feeling against it is still so strong that it is rare in spite of being easy. Sheep stray, they are not guarded all the time, and although each flock is ear-marked and wool-marked, the wool-marking washes off in time and the ear-marking can be altered by dog-bites, or, it has been said by a veterinary surgeon in court, by disease. When the sheep are gathered for shearing or dipping, the dogs and men always miss a sheep or two on the mountain.

Two farmers in Llan have been suspected of stealing sheep. Both were men from highly respected families, but even if they were not, I think the charge would be too grave for anyone to make openly against them. A case of sheep-stealing was taken to court in a town ten miles away from Llan in 1956, when two farmers sharing an open mountain with several other farmers were accused of shearing sheep belonging to the other farmers. The case aroused widespread interest and astonishment and no similar case can be recalled. An interesting point in this case was that one farmer said in court that he recognized the way one of his sheep had been sheared as the shearing of the accused.

Sheep stray often and if two farmers are friendly and one finds another's sheep on his land, he will return them as soon as he can, since there is a considerable risk that straying sheep will wander far afield and become completely lost. Otherwise he will inform the owner or send word to him. If the owner persistently refuses to move his sheep, the finder will resent his pasture being eaten by someone else's sheep and will threaten to shut them up and charge so much for the release of each sheep. Matters are rarely taken so far that sheep are actually shut up – the owner usually acts on this threat. In 1945 such a case arose in Llan and it was followed by a fight and then a court case; but the man who left his sheep on someone else's land for so long that they were shut up and then waited for the other farmer with a stick, was a dealer – a very different type from the ideal 'patriarch'.

Sheep-dogs are not only an excellent breed for working with sheep, but they are a breed which tends to chase and worry sheep. Puppies, before they are trained, will run after a field full of sheep and there is danger of the sheep drowning in the ditches that drain the flat land. Dogs that chased sheep while they were puppies may revert to worrying sheep in later life, especially if they have a companion. After chasing sheep, if they catch them in a narrow ditch, for instance, and bite them, they get the taste for the meat and after that will go on killing. Sheep-worrying is the case most likely to be taken to court. Sheep-stealing occurs rarely and the charge is too serious to make without absolute certainty and probably without some enmity between the parties. Sheep-straying occurs very frequently and is not so serious that it cannot be settled out of court, usually. Sheep-worrying occurs more often than stealing, does not entail a fault in a man's character greater than carelessness, and at the same time is so serious when sheep are actually dying that Llan people will take their neighbours to court over it. Even so, most cases I have heard or read of have been accusations against visitors' dogs, or, like one recent case in Llan between one Welsh and one English farmer, accusations involving farmers who had a long-standing feud between them.

In Llan parish, then, informal methods such as friendly compromise, fear of public opinion, the need to co-operate and finally ostracism, keep most disputes between people out of court, and if not an actual substitute for English justice, make English justice (costly as well as foreign) only a final and extreme resort.

CHAPTER SEVEN

CHAPEL AND CHURCH

THE themes of this chapter are, first, whether the church/chapel[1] division is the basis for the division of Llan people in other contexts; and second, the way in which, as the role of the chapel becomes less important in Welsh life and ceases to canalize their cultural tradition, this role is taken over by other institutions.

Llan's population of 241 adults may be divided into congregations[2] as follows:

Methodists	144
Baptists	19
Church	40
Others	18
Not known	20

The morality preached by the church is not different in practical application from that preached by the two Nonconformist groups, and the added intensity of moral fervour initiated during the Nonconformist revival which spread over North Wales in the nineteenth century is as effective on church

[1] For brevity's sake I shall sometimes use the term 'chapel' when I wish to refer to both Nonconformist congregations in Llan: Baptist and Methodist.

[2] By Methodists I mean Calvinistic Methodists. The figure given is the total number of people who, if asked their religion, would say 'Methodist' and the same may be said of the number of Baptists. Of the total number of Methodists, 109 are paid-up members. Of the total number of Baptists, 14 have been baptized and thus become full members, and five regularly attend the Baptist chapel and contribute to its funds. Since not all the church-goers attend Llan church, the precise number of those who are confirmed and therefore full members is not available. 'Others' include Catholics, Salvation Army members, members of the Independent chapel and those known to be atheists or agnostics.

as on chapel people now. It is all-pervading though weakened. Church people are as reluctant to gather hay on Sundays as are chapel people; just as disapproving in theory of illegitimacy as chapel people and just as kind in practice to the people involved when illegitimacy occurs. Roughly the same proportion of church people as chapel people drink, go dancing in the neighbouring towns when young, or gamble on the football pools and in other ways. One family of church members has had a reputation in the past for being peculiarly immoral. About this Z family it is said 'they used to marry their cousins', 'they were always in court', 'they were always having illegitimate children', 'Evan Z used to sleep with a married woman' and so on. I never heard their church membership quoted in connection with their immorality. They simply took the role of the 'bad family' in Llan. The very size of the family played its part – the founder of the Llan family had 15 children. Members of the second, third and fourth generations of the family who were brought up or born in the Z house still live in the parish. A look at the court and parish records shows that the Z family have been given their notoriety not by their exploits being exaggerated, but by similar and almost as numerous exploits by their fellow parishioners – church and chapel – being 'forgotten' – for the time being, while the Z's were under discussion. Morally, church and chapel people in Llan are undifferentiated.

Chapel activities are more extensive than are church activities: partly because for long the existence of a much larger congregation has made this possible; but also because, during the Nonconformist revival, when the chapel said 'no' to games, to drink, to work and play on Sundays, to dancing and to play-acting, it took over, amended and held under its own auspices, some secular entertainments which remained after the general 'stamping out'. However, most of the social events organized by the chapel, such as 'little concerts' in which children and adults in age groups from 4 to over 21 compete in solo singing, singing in harmony, recitation, baking, drawing and sight-reading tonic sol-fa, and discussion groups, are now attended by church, Methodist and Baptist people. Similarly, when the church holds whist drives and raffles to raise funds, the chapel people support them. Whist drives and raffles are 'gambling' and so the chapels as bodies cannot organize them. Nevertheless, chapel people like playing whist – indeed if they did not attend whist drives (which are organized by the Women's Institute, the youth club and other bodies as well as the church) no profit on them could possibly be realized.

Thus church and chapel people unite for all formal entertainments that are held in the parish or district, whether organized by themselves, as with the entertainments described above, or organized by other bodies such as the Women's Institute or the W.E.A. Similarly there are no religious divisions between them in informal entertainments and they act together as poachers and drinkers and go together on occasional outings to Liverpool, Manchester, the Isle of Man or Ireland, to shop, see motor-cycle races, or horse-races, or just to see 'sights'.

I have no evidence as to whether or not there is a correlation between people's politics and their religion in Llan. Elections to the parish council, rural district council and county council are not affected by political party or religious schisms; there is frequently only one candidate for each vacancy and when there is voting it is based on personal likings, kinship ties and personal appraisals of the candidates' worth.[1] There has been no case in this century of the church backing one candidate and either of the chapels backing another candidate in elections which have affected Llan. Indeed if this happened in elections for the parish council, since Methodists outnumber the other denominations, there would be only Methodists on the parish council. In fact churchmen and Baptists also sit on it.

The church congregation is so small that it would not be use-

---

[1] Trefor M. Owen, writing about the parish of Glan-llyn in Merioneth, which he studied in 1951, said: 'People will remark when local elections are being held, that all the Independents (or Methodists) will vote for the candidate who is a fellow-member, but after a few seconds' thought will also stress that such factors as the number of relatives, the farming or business connections and the political views and personal popularity of the candidates is likely to influence voters. Other things being equal, however, religious affiliation does count. . . .' I can find no evidence of a similar situation in Llan.

D. Jenkins and others, *Welsh Rural Communities*, Ed. E. Davies and A. D. Rees (Cardiff 1960).

ful to attempt to find the relative proportions of farmers, white-collared workers, quarrymen and other workers attending church and chapel. The Cwmparc family of gentry are church-goers; the Plas family attend neither church nor chapel. Beneath this social level, as explained in Chapter Four, Llan people are almost undifferentiated as far as social status is concerned, but no one occupation group is more associated with church than with chapel and the church congregation includes farmers, quarrymen and white-collared workers. In the past this was not the case. 'In England the different religious denominations cut across social divisions and to some degree neutralized them. . . . But in Wales social distinctions coincided with and were intensified by differences not only in religion but also in language. The gap between the tenant farmer and his landlord, who had become anglicized despite his pride in his long Welsh pedigree, was increased by the spread of nonconformity.'[1]

One hundred years ago, church meant 'English landlord' and chapel meant 'Welsh tenantry'. The main difference between church and chapel today is that the chapels are exclusively Welsh. All English people in Llan go to church if they go anywhere: they could hardly go to either of the chapels since proceedings there are entirely in the Welsh language. Church services are held in a mixture of Welsh and English. But for the Welsh-speaking church-goers, the fact that they attend church is not determined by class or political considerations. Their ancestors may have stayed in the church during the revival in fear of and in a desire to associate with the gentry; and they, the present generation, as they happen to have been born into the church are quite pleased to have the distinction of having the Cwmparc gentry in their congregation. But this distinction is not enough to attract other people, however status-seeking they may be, out of the chapels and into church.

The division of Llan people into three religious denominations is not relevant to the other divisions of Llan people to which I have referred so far. It remains to be asked whether the religious division causes Llan people to take sides in differences of opinion that arise spontaneously. A case of such a difference of opinion

[1] D. Williams, *A History of Modern Wales* (London 1950).

which I observed was over the formation and continued activity of a youth club in Dinas church hall for all young people in Llan. One of the various pessimistic comments made to me when the idea of the youth club was first discussed was the remark, 'A church clique will run it; and when they are tired of it, they will close it.'

A group of church people had started a club in the church hall in previous years, which had failed. The cessation of the club had not left the village unified: the end of the club bringing the end of quarrels about the club. The censure, an underground mumble, about who had failed in running the club and whose fault it was, continued after the club had closed down. Church-goers had played a prominent part in that venture and so were attacked for the behaviour of the youths who went to the club and for the failure of the club, but this was a temporary grouping, and when the new club opened it was replaced by a re-grouping on a different basis. For the reopening members of the Women's Institute, the vicar of Llan church and prominent members of chapel and church joined together. The youngsters who became members (chapel without exception) wanted above all somewhere to meet each other apart from the street, so that they could do so without their parents' complaints: they wanted to gossip, play, flirt and jive. Some elders were content to provide facilities for what the youngsters wanted, satisfied if they would accept adult supervision at all and arguing that school and homework provided enough work for the children. Some elders approved the formation of the club but wished to organize educational activities for the club meetings, even if the young people did not want them. Some elders disapproved of the club altogether and said that the youngsters were a noisy crowd, would not do what they were told, would wreck the hall and were not interested in anything; the girls attracted men from far and wide and it was impossible to run anything in Dinas. In this dispute, people did not take sides according to their religious affiliation, but according to their desire to acquire status in the village, and personal ability to tolerate noise and to sympathize with teenagers.

Another dispute which involved religious grouping to a certain extent was the case of the Women's Institute whist drive

Chapel and Church

which was almost held in Lent. Two groups of church people were involved. One group agreed to let the church hall to the Women's Institute on a date which happened to fall in Lent. The second group objected to this and village opinion rallied against the second group. The letting was cancelled; the whist drive had to be held in a neighbouring parish and it was not a success. Nevertheless, feeling in this dispute ran more along personal than along religious lines and the Women's Institute still includes church-goers among its members.

The church/chapel division is not the basis for the division of Llan people in other contexts. Not only have the quarrels between Anglicans and Nonconformists and between the founders of the various sects of Nonconformism in Wales been forgotten in Llan, but the divisions between them are not used to dress out new quarrels and divisions. The existence of the three denominations does not break up the unity of Llan people, who feel attached to a community far wider than the chapel or church: the Welsh-speaking community. Chapel-going is Welsh and so Llan people approve of chapel-going. But some members of the Baptist chapel go to the Methodist chapel and vice versa, because it is nearer, or because a friend goes. Chapel-going is Welsh but being religious generally is Welsh. So some people go to church regularly and to chapel for an occasional special service;[1] while some regular chapel-goers attend church once a year. In the main people belong to the denomination their parents belonged to. Of the six married couples in Llan of mixed religious denomination, the partners in three cases have continued, after marriage, to go to their

[1] Thanksgiving, a local term for Harvest Festival, is the most important service in the year: if those out of touch with religion will ever go to church or chapel, they will go on Thanksgiving Day. In some parishes the Methodist minister speaks in the church: in others joint services between the various denominations are held; in Llan many people like to attend the services in both church and chapel. This practice of swallowing denominational differences at Thanksgiving exists in various parts of rural England and clearly can be mainly accounted for by the importance of harvest time in rural areas. However, in North Wales, where denominational differences were even more bitter than they were in England 100 years ago, the practice should be seen in the light of the general toning down of differences in favour of the unity of Welsh-speaking people.

original places of worship. Loyalty to their own denomination and a desire to maintain links with two groups (pleasant socially and perhaps useful economically), are two of the motives involved. But as an equal number have changed their place of worship after marriage, it is clear that these motives are not general.

The second theme of this chapter is the way in which, as the chapel ceases to canalize the Welsh cultural tradition, this role is taken over by other institutions.

Beginning in roughly 1730, a Nonconformist revival swept Wales. In 1785 Baptist preachers visited Llan and nine adults were baptized in one of the mountain streams. Baptists met in a public house, in a carpenter's shed and in two farms and in 1787 a Baptist chapel was built. Robert Owen of Rhyl worked in the parish in 1818 and wrote 'The Baptists owned the whole parish from Carmel to Dinas. They were very staunch and you had to be very brave to be a Methodist at that time.'[1] But at the time he wrote, the membership of the Baptist church for the county as a whole numbered less than 300 and the Baptists never gained a large congregation. A local Baptist historian writes that the Baptists in Llan and in a neighbouring parish could not have numbered together more than 35 in 1880 and were 150 in 1912. These few people built or bought four chapels and paid for them a total of £3,290. One of the four chapels was the new Baptist chapel in Llan, built with the stones of the old one, in 1904.

The Methodists came to Llan in 1796 and started a Sunday school in a farm-house. The four Methodist chapels which still stand in Llan were originally built in 1833, 1863, 1872 and 1904.

Before the revival, religion meant very little in the lives of the North Welsh people. The church, English-speaking and for most of its incumbents merely a source of income, was reformed too late. It was the Nonconformist church, and in the main Congregationalist Methodism, which won the North Welsh people from what had been described as their dark superstition. The impetus of the revival lasted well into the period between the two world wars and young people in Llan can remember

[1] R. Owen, *Hanes Methodistiaeth Gorllewin Meirionydd*, 1891.

the usually empty roads and paths of the parish black with people flocking to a preaching festival. On such occasions, the Baptist chapel, usually two-thirds empty, would be so full that benches were put outside to seat the overflow; and similar scenes occurred in all the chapels.

The chapels took over much of the Welsh culture and forced it into new channels. In the Sunday schools which sprang up everywhere, and which were described as the 'main instrument of civilization in North Wales'[1] adults and children learnt how to read and write Welsh; and from reading the Bible they could go on to reading their own poets. 'Their schools, literature and religious pursuits . . . have cultivated talents for preaching and poetry,' wrote the Education Commissioners, going on: 'but for every other calling they are incapacitated.' The fire-side story-tellers, the tellers and actors of dramatic interludes, became eloquent preachers and lay leaders of spontaneous prayer at prayer meetings. To the repertoire of Welsh folk song was added a large and fine collection of hymns in the Welsh language. Trefor M. Owen, writing about Glan-llyn says that, the chapel when it turned people against dancing, games, acting and drinking and took over for its own uses the conversational and musical talents of the Welsh, restricted 'the secular recreation to that which is indirectly connected with the work on the farm such as the fair and the shearing party.'[2] This is not quite true: Eisteddfodau under other auspices than those of the chapel have been held in Wales throughout the last and the present century, and these, nationally, regionally and locally, attracted much artistic talent into secular channels. The public houses always kept alive the art of singing and story-telling outside the chapels. Some things peculiarly Welsh, such as the attitude towards sexual matters, and the old courting habits, continued throughout the revival hardly touched. Nevertheless the chapel was for a hundred years the main symbol of Welshness in every rural parish in North Wales.

In many countries colonized by Europeans the people have

[1] Report of Commissioners of Inquiry into the State of Education in Wales, 1847.
[2] D. Jenkins and others, *Welsh Rural Communities*, Ed. E. Davies & A. D. Rees (Cardiff 1960).

expressed the tensions so produced by religious or mystical movements which share many of the characteristics of the Welsh revival. Natives of Melanesia had fits after 'hearing the voice of God on the telephone'; natives of North Wales spoke of holy music in the air. Africans danced themselves into a trance at religious meetings; Welsh people listening to Howell Harris in the 1740s leaped and jumped for joy, clapping their hands and crying 'Halleluia!'' for hours after the sermon until they fell to the ground exhausted.

Discrimination between white and black in Christian churches in Africa, North America and elsewhere has led to the founding of separatist churches by the coloured people and these churches have the three functions of first, giving the coloured people opportunities for leadership; secondly, combining Christian and native beliefs and customs; and thirdly, acting as vehicles for anti-white feelings either by Utopian prophecies, as when the Watch Tower prophets in Rhodesia preached of the day when Europeans would become slaves of Africans, or by working under the slogan 'Africa for the Africans', and setting up native land-buying syndicates and exhorting the congregations to buy property.

In like manner the Nonconformist chapels in North Wales gave Welshmen opportunities for leadership which had been denied them since Henry VIII's Act of Union; it combined Christian beliefs with the use of the Welsh language; and it acted as a vehicle for the growth of national consciousness in a previously non-unified country.

The awakening of the Welsh people to a feeling that they were a nation took first a predominantly religious form and then became a movement which was religious and political at the same time. Whilst the early dissenters, the Independents and Baptists, were politically active, supported Chartism and defended the Rebecca Rioters when they destroyed toll-gates; the Methodists were numerically far stronger and they condemned trade unionism and forbade their members to become Chartists. In the latter half of the nineteenth century, however, the Methodists joined with the older dissenters to form a strong radical political force. In the general election of 1859 landowners in Merioneth evicted tenants who voted for the Nonconformist candidate. In 1860 'a Cardiganshire land-owner informed her tenants that they must either become members of the Church of England or leave her estate'.[1] Nonconformist religion and radical politics were closely linked and largely carried Welsh culture, especially education and language, with them.

In many parts of the world, religious or mystical movements on the one hand and political movements on the other hand have been alternative methods of reacting to oppression: the irrational and the rational. In the long run the two do prove generally to be incompatible and in Wales, though for a time religion and politics became united rather than alternative forms of protest, the political movement outgrew the religious one and the bonds between culture, religion and politics broke. Politically the Welsh joined the working-class struggle as the right to strike and the minimum wage took the place of toll-gates and tithes as issues of the day. The miners and quarrymen took most of the farmers, farm-workers and the few non-anglicized white-collared workers with them when they returned first Liberal and then Labour Party members to Parliament from most Welsh constituencies.

In religious matters the Welsh people, while never so in-different as the English, became less and less fervent. Attendances in Dinas chapel are sometimes so low that services are held in the vestry; six people attend the Baptist chapel regularly, one of whom comes from outside the parish.

The scene of Welsh cultural life moved and is still moving from the chapel to the day schools, W.E.A. classes, the public houses, the fairs held on traditional hiring fair dates, the meetings of Women's Institutes and the informal meetings of villagers. The close ties in the past between Welsh culture, religion and politics have led some religious people to hope for a revival of Welsh culture by means of specifically Welsh politics. They believe that the weakening of the chapel is a sign that Welsh culture is moribund. The Welsh Nationalist Party 'Plaid Cymru' is a movement of people who despair of the Welsh culture surviving and see political separatism as the only remedy. Their programme speaks of economics, but far greater

[1] D. Williams, *A History of Modern Wales* (London 1950).

importance is given in all their propaganda and certainly by Llan members to the saving of Welsh culture. In Llan, most of those who vote for the Plaid are regular chapel-goers and teetotallers: people who might be regarded as 'buchedd A'[1] were it not that they prefer their sons to dig ditches rather than to leave Wales, and that they go poaching with the rest. They do not see that the strength of the chapel is no longer a measure of the strength of the culture. Teenagers of today go through a phase of Americanization but they do not forget the Welsh songs and poems, though it is too early to tell which they will eventually choose. In a public house in Caernarvon in recent years young men competed in hurling at each other insulting verses which they composed on the spot: thus continuing a centuries-old tradition. In so far as they act politically the North Welsh act together with the rest of the British working class although they are not very conscious of being part of it; their interest in religious questions has declined; but there are many signs that the culture is still alive. The growing interest in National Eisteddfodau is one such sign. Improved transport means that more people can attend the 'national' than ever before and the book of the National Eisteddfod, which gives the judgements and criticisms of the written entries, is in great demand, those who have bought it lending it around. There are countless local and regional eisteddfodau and Llan people are unanimous in according respect to winners in these competitions: whatever personal or moral failings they may have. Shearing parties and hiring fairs with the eisteddfodau continued as secular carriers of tradition throughout the revival and still flourish. And the repertoire of Welsh hymns, folk songs and poetry which can be heard in the public houses is perhaps the surest sign that Welsh culture is not dead.

[1] A classification which is explained in Chapter One, page 11.

CHAPTER EIGHT

THE ROLE OF 'NOT KNOWING' IN THE MORAL CODE

THE chapel in North Wales has more influence on people's lives than has church or chapel on the lives of people in South England. In both districts, extra-marital sexual relations and the birth of illegitimate children are disapproved in churches and Nonconformist chapels alike.

In the working-class districts of London where, between 1930 and 1950, I grew up, it was said that a girl who became pregnant would be turned out of her home by her parents, and this threat was taken so seriously that such girls left home. There are far more unmarried mothers in North Wales than in London working-class districts and the girls invariably stay at home. No individual, mother or neighbour, 'casts them out', although the chapel as a body did until recently. It is interesting that all but four of England's thirty-nine counties have hostels or homes for unmarried mothers and their children; while of Wales's thirteen counties, only Glamorganshire in the industrial south is so provided.[1] The lack of hostels is no proof that they are not required; but the local evidence strongly suggests that there is no demand for them in North Wales. Pregnant girls in Llan are met with such tolerance at home that they do not feel they have to leave. There is a sense in which it is true to say that they could not do so. In large towns, anonymity is a phenomenon familiar to all. Everyone knows that it is possible, by moving a very little distance, to live and work among people to whom one is a perfect stranger. Such a move is a feasible alternative in people's minds to 'sticking out trouble' at home. In the minds

[1] *Directory of Homes and Hostels for the Care of Unmarried Mothers and Illegitimate Children*, published by the National Council for the Unmarried Mother and her Child, 1956 edition, with 1959 amendments.

101

of Llan people such a move has not been a feasible proposition, and in fact such a move would be for them more expensive, more risky, and more completely an upheaval than it would be for a town girl. Thus, to a certain extent, Llan is obliged to face the illegitimacy in its midst. However, the same thing could be said about any remote country district; yet such tolerance as is found in Llan is not found in all remote country districts of Great Britain, and unmarried mothers from all parts of England and Ireland leave their homes and travel to large cities to have their babies. I should be very surprised to learn of a Llan mother taking such a step.

I should make it clear that the relatively high rate of illegitimacy in North Wales is not a recent phenomenon coinciding with the decline in attendance at chapel. Indeed it can be seen from the graph on page 109 that the figures for Merioneth and for Llan's rural district are coming closer to the figure for England and Wales as a whole and such evidence as there is for more recent years suggests that the gap is narrowing still further.

The important role that the chapel still plays in North Welsh people's lives has not meant that they have adopted the chapel code as their moral code. Generally people adhere more closely to their own moral code[1] than they do to the code of behaviour laid down by their religious organization. Public opinion in Llan has not been changed with regard to illegitimacy and from the width of the gap between the firm 'no' that chapel and church say to fornication and illegitimacy on the one hand and the extent to which both are practised in North Wales on the other, it can be seen that the North Welsh do not really think them wrong.

The Rev. J. W. Trevor, chaplain to the Lord Bishop of Bangor, wrote in 1847: 'I assert with confidence, as an undeniable fact, that fornication is not regarded as a vice, scarcely as a frailty, by the common people in Wales. It is considered as a matter of course – as the regular conventional process towards

---

[1] By 'moral code' I mean here not an individual's code but matters of right and wrong which are agreed upon in the community and which, though slow to change, are more adaptable than codes laid down by religious organizations.

marriage. . . . When I attempted at the Union Board to persuade the guardians to build a workhouse (we have none in Anglesey), and used as an argument that it would check the increase of bastardy, which is a monstrous charge on our poor rates, as well as a disgrace to our community, they quite scouted the notion of its being any disgrace, and they maintained that the custom of Wales justified the practice.'

The above was written[1] at a time when people all over North Wales were fired with the religious enthusiasm of the Methodist Revival. For periods of several years in succession, in hamlets and parishes all over the district, people 'heard holy music in the air'; congregations shouted and leaped for joy.

The whole report of the Commissioners of Inquiry into the State of Education in Wales, and especially the preponderance of evidence from Anglicans, has been severely criticized. The critics were quite correct when they said that illegitimacy rates were at that time higher for parts of Scotland and Northern England than they were for North Wales, but this did not extricate them from the difficulty that North Wales's rate was still higher than average. And in 1950, the Merioneth rate, at 10·2 per cent, was the highest for any county in England and Wales.

Twenty-seven of my population of 346 people living in Llan in 1959 were illegitimate, and eight illegitimate children of Llan people are being brought up or are living outside the parish. When a girl has an illegitimate baby in Llan, disapproval is expressed to her by her family, and about her by others when she and her family are out of hearing. Of the twenty-seven, twenty-four were born to Methodist mothers, two to Baptist mothers and one to a church mother, and in all but the latter case and the most recent chapel case, the chapels took discriminatory action by turning the mother away from chapel meetings for a time. Although the chapels, both Methodist and Baptist, have acted as a body in the past to reject the mother of an illegitimate child, the families concerned generally return to the congregation. They may cease to pay subscriptions but they still regard themselves as Methodists or Baptists and will return,

[1] To the Commissioners of Inquiry into the State of Education in Wales.

if only to attend Thanksgiving services or special preaching festivals. The possible alternative of joining the church is one that is not taken.

It often happens that the child is reared entirely by his maternal grandmother, in ignorance as to who his true mother is: he addresses his grandmother as his mother, and his mother as his sister; although almost invariably his friends at school know the true situation and sooner or later will enlighten him. This has happened in Llan and I know of cases in neighbouring parishes where it is happening now. Four of the illegitimate children living in Llan were or are being brought up mainly by their maternal grandparents. This happens more often when the father is unknown or when it seems certain that the father will not marry the mother, either because he is married already, as in one case, or because he lives far away or for some similar reason. The mothers then have a better chance of finding a husband.

Children brought up by their grandparents are not by this fact conspicuously illegitimate, since three legitimate children are being reared by their grandparents and it is quite common for children in North Wales to be reared by or at least borrowed by aunts or grandparents. In two of the cases, both parents are alive and living near by. In the third, the mother is divorced from her husband and her mother looks after her son, while she goes to work.

Neither being illegitimate nor having had an illegitimate child has been a bar to marriage in Llan.[1]

I have suggested that Llan people deviate from the chapel code not only in the matter of illegitimacy but also in extra-marital sexual association generally. Alwyn Rees writes that the fact of illegitimacy rates being high 'must not be regarded as evidence of greater laxity in rural areas than in modern com-

[1] Of the twenty-one women living in Llan who had illegitimate children, nine have married, two are still very young and are likely to marry, two were widows when they became pregnant. Of the twenty-seven people living in Llan who were born illegitimate, only one seems to have grown to an age where she is unlikely to marry. The rest are either married or of an age where they are likely to marry. There seems some evidence that the choice of marriage partners in some cases is limited, since three of the mothers of illegitimate children have married men who were illegitimate.

munities generally'. He goes on: 'Effective means of contraception which are better known and more easily procurable in towns than in the countryside, have rendered statistics of this kind valueless for comparing extra-marital sexual life of urban and rural communities. The incidence of illegitimacy per thousand unmarried women aged 15–45 in England and Wales as a whole fell by about one half between 1890 and 1939, but it can hardly be said that this reflects a corresponding increase in continence.'[1]

Within that period, however, a drop of one half also occurred in the Merioneth rate of illegitimate births per thousand unmarried women aged 15–45; but the absolute level of Merioneth was still 50 per cent higher than that for England and Wales as a whole. Although it is possible, it seems very unlikely that half the increase in contraceptive knowledge occurred in Merioneth as that which occurred in England and Wales as a whole, and that uneven spread of that knowledge resulted in the relation between Merioneth and England and Wales being the same at the end as at the beginning of the period.

Taken by itself, the illegitimacy rate is clearly not a correct guide to the frequency of extra-marital sexual relations. Prostitution in towns allows much extra-marital activity with hardly any corresponding illegitimacy. But the existence of prostitution in the larger towns cannot appreciably affect the lowness of the illegitimacy rate for the whole of England and Wales as compared with that of Merioneth.

Similarly, Rees's point does not affect the Merioneth situation.

A third factor which may cause changes in the illegitimacy rate to take place without similar changes taking place in the incidence of extra-marital relations has been mentioned by Virginia Wimperis.[2] She quotes the Registrar-General in his statistical review of England and Wales for 1940–1945, where he points out that during the 1939–45 war, although the illegitimacy rate rose steeply, the rate of premarital pregnancies did not. The cause of the rise in illegitimacy was probably not due, therefore, to an increase in extra-marital associations, but to a drop in the number of women who, having conceived out of

[1] A. D. Rees, *Life in a Welsh Countryside* (Cardiff 1950).
[2] V. Wimperis, *The Unmarried Mother and Her Child* (London 1960).

wedlock, were able to marry before the child was born. This was due to call-up, separations and other abnormal conditions of the Second World War. Occurrences of this kind make it unwise to account for sudden changes in time in the illegitimacy rates by referring to increased or decreased extra-marital associations.

However, in North Wales, and certainly in Llan, both illegitimacy and pre-marital conceptions have been consistently high as compared to England and Wales for many years. I think that when there are such consistent differences between one place and another; and when the objections mentioned above have been taken into account (i.e. prostitution, contraception and the rate of pre-marital conceptions) then a relatively high rate of illegitimacy can be seen as evidence of a relatively high occurrence of extra-marital relationships.

In addition to the high rate of illegitimacy there is further evidence to show that the incidence of extra-marital sexual relations is significantly far from the continence prescribed by church and chapel.

The Welsh people used to court in bed: sometimes with a bolster interposed and sometimes with nothing but faith between the courting couple. A traveller in 1811 describes the practice as declining then.[1] It is clear from the Report of the Royal Commission on Land in Wales and Monmouthshire[2] that such 'night courtship' still survived in 1893 and Rees, who did most of his field work during the 1939–45 war, wrote that the custom still survived then in the part of North Wales in which he worked.[3] I have no evidence as to whether or not this custom still prevails in Llan, but courting in Llan, whether in bed or on the mountainside, is often productive, since the following figures show that a large proportion of marriages in Llan took place after the conception of the first child. Of my population of 346 the Welsh members had experienced ninety-four marriages.[4] To nine of these no children were born. For

[1] E. Hyde Hall, *A Description of Caernarvonshire, 1809–1811*. Ed. E. Gwynne Jones (Caernarvon 1952).

[2] Report of the Royal Commission on Land in Wales and Monmouthshire, 1896.

[3] A. D. Rees, *Life in a Welsh Countryside* (Cardiff 1950).

[4] I use this term because if I said 'number of people married' I would be almost doubling the number of marriages by counting both partners.

twenty-three of these I have insufficient information. Of the remaining sixty-two marriages, twenty-five, or 40 per cent, were followed by the birth of a child within eight months or less. Of eighty-six marriages registered locally as taking place between 1895 and 1959 in which one or both partners lived in Llan and in which children could be traced as being born in the parish, thirty-eight, or 44 per cent, were followed by the birth of a child within eight or less months. In 1950 the percentage of children born within eight or less months after their parents' marriage was 25·7 per cent in Wales II[1] as compared to the figures for England and Wales of 20.4: and for London and the South East 15.5. Wales II had the highest figure of the eleven regions into which England and Wales are divided by the Registrar General.[2] Descriptions of weddings in the local newspaper often omit the date of the ceremony and a chapel deacon apologized for the paucity of his records, explaining that few couples were willing to have dates of marriages and births recorded in the chapel's books.

Prostitutes are virtually unknown in North Wales, but a substitute exists and for young men whose sweethearts are virtuous, for bachelors and for others whose desires are not satisfied by monogamy, there is the institution of the 'good thing'. A 'good thing' is a lady, she may be a widow, a spinster or married, she may be in her teens or in her sixties or anywhere in between, who has a reputation for allowing easy access to her bed. She does not allow access to all and she will favour now one, now another man; she may have a permanent lover to whom she has borne children; if she has only one lover she is not a 'good thing'; to be in that category it must be worth the while of any man to try his luck with her. There is no question of money payment. Fifty years ago the 'good thing' was helped out by a visiting farmer with a sack of flour or potatoes; or by her landlord with easy terms of rent. In towns, nowadays, she may be treated to a few drinks. In the country, her permanent lover, if she has one, may help support her. But her acceptance or

[1] Wales II comprises Anglesey, Caernarvon, Cardigan, Denbigh, Flint, Merioneth, Montgomery, Pembroke and Radnor.
[2] Registrar General. *Statistical Review of England and Wales, Part II. Civil*, 1950.

refusal of most visitors will not depend upon gifts. Young men pass on addresses of 'good things' to each other and an informal 'wild set' exists over the whole district whose members co-operate to provide each other with up-to-date information. A young man gains gradual entrance to this set by showing that he is 'ready for anything', is 'quite a boy', a 'hen foy bach'. A man usually visits a 'good thing' outside his parish. Public opinion in North Wales was outraged by the statement by an Anglican churchman, the Rev. J. W. Trevor, whose evidence to the Education Commissioners I have already quoted, that in North Wales people had sexual intercourse in the presence of friends or relations. However, even now, after more than a century of Methodism, young men in North Wales do go in groups to visit 'good things' at times and since Wales is far from being the only place where such scenes occur, it is only unfortunate that some Englishmen and some churchmen should have implied that in this Wales was unique.

Before I go on to discuss the mechanism by which Llan people reconcile their adherence to church or chapel with their deviations from the codes of these institutions, it is worth asking, why these deviations? 'Fiddling' from officials and 'milking' English tourists can be explained in terms of the class war, but why is illegitimacy so high in Merioneth and why are so many marriages 'forced'?

There are three related topics: the high rate of illegitimacy; the large number of 'forced marriages'; and the late age of marriage.

The graphs show how the age of marriage of men in Llan is significantly higher than that of men in England and Wales as a whole; and the close association between age at marriage and rates of illegitimacy in Merionethshire and in the rural district in which the parish of Llan lies.

Rees relates the late age of marriage to inheritance of property and writes that the old people keep the farms going and the young people do not marry because they are waiting to inherit the farms. In Llan few farmers own their own farms; more important, a large percentage of the adult male population are not farmers' sons and had no stock, land or other property to expect.

A high rate of illegitimacy has been said variously to co-exist

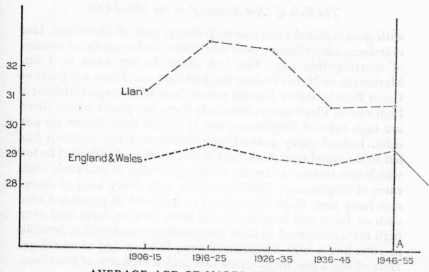

AVERAGE AGE OF MALES AT MARRIAGE.

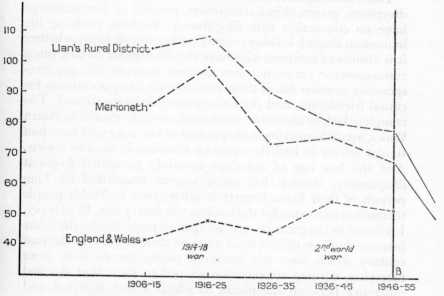

ILLEGITIMATE BIRTHS PER 1,000 LIVE BIRTHS

Points to the right of line A, B are for the three years 1956–57–58. At the time of preparation later figures were not available and these points do not have the same weight as the points in the main parts of the curves.

with geographical remoteness, poverty, lack of diversions, late marriage, a hot climate, poor education, and a surplus of women of marriageable age. The last three do not exist in Llan, Merioneth or North Wales; the first four do. There are parts of Great Britain and of Europe where these factors exist without a high rate of illegitimacy. Similarly there are places where there are high rates of illegitimacy but in which these factors do not exist. Indeed every general consideration of the problem has led to the conclusion that there is no simple and sufficient factor which can be seen to be the cause, generally, of relatively high rates of illegitimacy. Holiday resorts with every kind of diversion have high illegitimacy rates in England at present. Cities such as Paris and Stockholm, far from remote, have had very high rates compared to their surrounding countrysides. Norfolk in 1870 had a high illegitimacy rate, but low age of marriage. Ireland has a low illegitimacy rate and a high age of marriage.

These facts do not necessarily mean that lack or presence of diversions, geographical remoteness, poverty or late marriage have no connection with illegitimacy. Without studying life in modern English holiday resorts, it is impossible to say whether it is visitors or residents who have the illegitimate babies, but a common-sense connection can be seen between the gay irresponsible summer life of those resorts, with its opportunities for casual friendships, and the unfortunate births mentioned. The complete lack of diversion which until recently existed in North Wales, apart from visits to chapel and to kin, may well have had similar effects as had the opposite situation in seaside resorts. And the late age of marriage certainly permitted frequent illegitimacy, since it left many women unmarried for long periods of their lives. Poverty is often given by Welsh people themselves as a cause for the tendency to marry late. If, in reply, I referred to the great poverty and, more particularly, the acute housing shortage of industrial areas at various times in the past century which have not hindered young people there from marrying, ensuing conversation seemed to show that the real difference between the places to which I was referring and North Wales, was the relative attractiveness of the ideal of marriage. Welsh men, in particular, have been reluctant to marry; and have not seen marriage as a romantic partnership.

Indeed there is something anti-romantic in the North Welsh idea of human relationships. Rees writes, 'One seldom sees unmarried couples going for walks together . . . courtship is a private matter which has no public expression. Young couples usually behave nonchalantly towards each other in public and seldom acknowledge their friendship at social gatherings.'[1] This is still the general form of behaviour in Llan. In Llan most marriages take place without ceremony in a registry office. Partly this is due to many of the marriages being 'necessary' but partly it is due to the ceremony not having romantic associations.[2] There have been two cases in Llan in the last thirty years, of women pretending to be pregnant, and putting pillows under their clothes, in the hope of persuading some particular man to marry them. So I cannot extend this reluctance to marry to women. But side by side with the reluctance of the men to marry, has been a traditionally permissive attitude towards sexual matters. From the Ordinance of Rhuddlan, promulgated by Edward I in 1285, it is clear that the Welsh customary law allowed illegitimate sons to inherit land and property from their fathers, equally with legitimate sons. The application of English laws and the contrary teaching of the Methodist Revival hardly touched the practice of Welsh-speaking people in this matter. The figures for Llan for the past fifty years are consistent with the suggestion that men there have been reluctant to marry in their early youth, and have been able to find sexual partners without marrying. When pregnancy has followed intercourse, some of the young men have been persuaded to marry, thus contributing to the high figure for 'forced marriages' and other have evaded the pressures put on them to marry and thus fathered illegitimate children. Also consistent with this view would be the recent changes. Age at marriage has been dropping towards the average age at marriage for England and Wales as a whole. Similarly the illegitimacy rate has been dropping towards the rate for England and Wales as a whole. The geographical remoteness of North Wales is declining; her cultural traditions are at last meeting an attack which is

[1] A. D. Rees, *Life in a Welsh Countryside* (Cardiff 1950).
[2] People trying to climb the English prestige ladder emulate English courting customs and tend to get married in white with ceremony.

affecting them strongly; and there is some evidence in Llan that the idea of marriage as a romantic partnership between two young people has been infiltrating North Welsh society, via comics, magazines, films and generally closer contact with England and English ideas. Two young couples have been seen courting openly. The Llan family is not the 'economic unit of consumers' which the family in other parts of Great Britain is, according to the suggestion of Michael Young:[1] shopping and paying 'clubs' are the woman's affair; the man gives his wife 'housekeeping money', keeps some of his wages for himself and spends his share on tobacco, drink and transport. Nevertheless, some young married couples are seen in the local pub, drinking together, which is a very novel sight for Llan.

Illegitimacy, 'good things', the married women who are visited by bachelors, the spinsters who are visited by married men, the men who have slept with a girl and also with her mother, the poaching, the 'fiddling', the lack of respect for the property of large organizations, State Departments and Englishmen: everyone knows about these things. People are naturally curious and in the country their main source of entertainment and instruction is each other's behaviour. Most of those who participate go to church or chapel. How are these things reconciled with Llan people's verbal adherence to the chapel code? I ask this not with the implication 'How can such religious people be just as immoral as other people and be happy in their minds about it?' Such reconciling has to take place in most human groups. It is a well-nigh universal attribute of mankind that lip-service be paid to moralities which are not respected in action. The Welsh method of reconciling word and action may be analogous to others.

I have explained in Chapter One that there is not a chapel way of life and a public-house way of life, separate and distinct in Llan. There is a common set of values which includes everything considered to be typically Welsh. The hard drinkers and bad livers assume that respect is due to a chapel deacon and expect the deacons to live lives which the drinkers themselves would describe as 'better' than their own. The chapel code is clear in

[1] M. Young, *The Chipped White Cups of Dover*, Unit 2. Distributed by Observer Ltd.

people's minds and everyone pays lip-service to it. Young men
who have served in the forces and who have learnt of the other
and cynical values which exist among young men in other parts
of the British Isles, sing hymns in the pubs, when milking, at
open-air hymn singings on the beach, and in their homes, just
as do old men; and still refer unselfconsciously to the Bible in
argument. The 'bad' swear-words are the blasphemies: 'Great
Lord', 'By Hell', 'Great Bishop', 'Jesus Christ', 'Devil Hell';
which have become outdated in England because they no longer
attack anything sacred. In North Wales, religion is still important
enough for blasphemy to be 'bad'. The gloom of a Welsh Sunday
is notorious throughout Great Britain. Public houses are closed.
Very little work is done outside on Sundays and those who are
seen working are criticized strongly. A Llan farmer of Methodist
family, who has not been inside the chapel for many years, was
genuinely afraid that something awful would happen to him
after he had carried hay on a Sunday in a very wet year.

After Bob Glo had warned Bill Williams and Elwyn Jones
against mending one of Elwyn's cowsheds on Sundays, a cow on
Elwyn's farm died. Later, in the local pub, Elwyn threatened to
hit Bob Glo for 'witching' the job.

In most houses, Bibles, New Testaments, hymn books and
commentaries on the Bible form the bulk of permanent reading-
matter available.

But if every individual in Llan, whether chapel-goer or not,
subscribes to the chapel code, it is also true that every individual
in Llan approves some breaches of the chapel code.

No one manages to be a fully fledged puritan and indeed the
consistent puritan is rare everywhere. But the North Welsh
have a system of double values which in some respects is
peculiar to themselves. They not only fail to live up to the chapel
code but they admire certain breaches of it and their system of
values gives equal though different importance to the clever
poacher and the deacon. It is not a question of the chapel people
being on one side of the fence and the rogues on the other. I
have been told about some of the outstanding scandals of the
parish by an old chapel deacon and a virtuous, middle-aged,
chapel-going housewife, and both of them spoke with a note of
admiration in their voices which they scarcely bothered to try

to disguise. 'The rogues are Welsh; they do not divorce their wives and go away from the parish with someone else as we think English people would do. They are immoral in a Welsh way. They go to chapel on Thanksgiving Day like everyone else, speak respectfully to those older than themselves, are shocked if a deacon swears, and go to their assignations secretly, with their tracks well covered.' This is the unspoken commentary by which the parishioners condone behaviour which the chapel condemns.

The majority of Llan people lead quiet and respectable lives, are faithful to their husbands and wives and do nothing very scandalous.

The deacon who got drunk and the deacon who was forced to marry did their very best to hide it. Nevertheless, there are not two distinct ways of life; there are not two separate and conflicting communities as Davies and Rees suggest there are generally in Welsh parishes.[1] There are not two mutually exclusive ways of being Welsh. Points are given to the poet, the clever evader of officials, the deacon, the well-read man, the 'devil with the girls', so long as the poetry is Welsh, the well-read man has read Welsh books, the 'devil' and the 'fiddler' get up to their tricks in a Welsh way.

Yet there is a great rift between the way people are supposed to behave according to chapel code and the way they do behave, partly because their moral code is not identical with the chapel code. I can think of no Welsh person in the parish who would not associate himself with chapel or church, even if he does not in fact pay a subscription or even attend Thanksgiving services, but some people are closer to the chapel than others, and some really disapprove of loose morals, for instance, whilst others only pretend to disapprove. One person's moral code clashes with another person's moral code and, similarly, some behaviour may be morally acceptable to a person but will clash with his stated acceptance of the chapel code. If people are to live harmoniously with each other and, indeed, with themselves, they must pretend not to know half of what they do know about each other. In this pretence they are well schooled. I have often

[1] E. Davies and A. D. Rees, *Introduction to Welsh Rural Communities* (Cardiff 1960).

thought the first sentence a North Welsh child learns to say is 'Dwn im' – 'I don't know'.[1] It is the automatically given response to almost every question. Apart from the fact that politeness demands that he should 'not know', the Welsh person has another reason for 'not knowing'. He does not want to commit himself. If he stalls long enough, expresses surprise at each piece of information given to him by the man who is talking to him, he hopes he will find out more and more from the speaker and thus be in a better position versus that man if it comes to making a bargain, and *vis-à-vis* the world generally.

'It is customary to approach subjects which are in any way personal in an extremely circuitous manner, and direct questions play a much smaller part than in modern life. The usual method is to lead the conversation round to a point where the desired information is relevant to the discussion, perhaps as a confirmation or a contradiction of the view expressed by one of of the company.'[2] I have seen a child of 7 using this method skilfully in an attempt to win information from me without asking for it: that is without appearing to want it.

The equivalent game in many English town circles is just the opposite. In spite of the Englishman's reputation for modesty which exists in some parts of the world (perhaps mainly in England), to the North Welshman, and perhaps to countrymen generally, the town Englishman seems to wish to give the impression that he knows everything. He bursts into Llan pub and in two minutes has mentioned all the gossip he knows to the people in there.

'You were up late this morning, Gwil.'

'X came back from Leeds early. Wasn't she supposed to be staying for a month?' and so on.

[1] Life in any small community would be extremely difficult without this kind of pretence. Elizabeth Colson confirms this: 'I found myself . . . understanding perfectly why they frequently answered my questions with "I don't know. I never asked." . . . I learned that this was the best and only protection against the love of gossip, probably common to most small villages where news and comment upon it quickly travels the length of the village and back again. The quickest way to create a lack of response was to seem to be prying into someone's personal affairs.' Elizabeth Colson, *The Makah Indians* (Manchester 1958).

[2] A. D. Rees, *Life in a Welsh Countryside* (Cardiff 1950).

He has spent his capital of knowledge immediately and trusts that the interest will come in quickly – people will think: 'A man who knows so much might just as well know the rest.' This is mad squandering to the Llan man, whose great gambit is to lay out nothing: to gain without investing. To foreigners he is dumb – he knows absolutely nothing. He has just come from the river where he saw the water was far too low for salmon and is told:

'Plenty of salmon about now, Huw. I saw some big ones up by the bridge.'

'Oh, yes,' he replies. 'Duw, that's good'.

Told that the trouble with his car is that the plugs are not sparking, when he has seen the broken gasket with his own eyes, he will agree with his English 'know-all' adviser and may go to the point of testing the plugs before he 'discovers' the broken gasket. He will play-act the part of the country bumpkin and will find things out by attending to conversations which the speakers think could mean nothing to him. His is the partisan's approach – not the open attack but the subtlety of underground warfare.

To the outer circle of his acquaintance, the Llan man will still play the 'I don't know' game. It is his way of doing business to pretend not to know current prices, to pretend not to be interested in the deal and then suddenly to floor his opponent by a casual reference to the age or inferior udder of the beast in question or a reference to a very low price which X had to accept at Dolgellau the day before. It is also his way of acquiring most information in the gossip game. He knows a certain amount about the court case twenty miles away in which Twm Glo of Aber is concerned but he is sure that if he pretends to know nothing his informant will feel obliged to tell him the whole story as far as she knows it; and will include details new to him. She will talk, if she does, because someone has got to give in, because some are more talkative and more tempted to tell a story than others, and perhaps because she includes him in a closer circle to herself than he would think her, and perhaps because the topic is one on which she does not mind talking to almost anyone, whereas it may be one which he would reserve for a closer circle.

It is only to his near relatives and most intimate friends that the Llan man will tell all he knows. Gossip is the commodity which is exchanged most in country life: it is the currency of social relationships and the Llan man saves it up to help himself and his relatives: he does not scatter it (or real money) abroad as does the 'mad' Englishman.

In matters of morality and religion, this partisan lifemanship game is useful. People do their best 'not to know' and not to let others know about breaches of the chapel code. A farmer who was also a deacon, who wanted some work done quickly, said to his employees, when they suggested working on a Sunday, 'No one will see you on your way up to the mountain if you go early'. The practice of 'not knowing' enables North Welsh people to live with their 'sins'. It must be taken into account if much of their behaviour is to be understood. It helps to explain, for instance, why, in their value system, divorce is unthinkable. Divorce would be an open breach; a public admission of failure; a way of tackling a problem quite foreign to the whole 'Welsh' way of doing things which I have tried to describe. It may seem remarkable that a community whose public policy so depends upon a respectable exterior should be able to accommodate a large number of illegitimate children, amongst other irregularities, in its midst. It is precisely the way in which Llan's policy of 'not knowing' meets this challenge which shows that policy in all its subtlety and efficiency. In general conversation, ages of eldest children become hazy; the month in which a marriage took place is not named; kinship terms are not used with any precision: 'cousin' covers many relationships; 'brother' includes half-brother. When a dangerous topic approaches, the speakers become more and more vague about which side of the family the link is traceable through, and conclude that 'there's some sort of relationship'. But if the discussion is on kinship specifically, and the questioner clearly knows many of the true facts, then the conversation will become very precise; providing no one is present who is personally involved in any 'irregularity' and who would be embarrassed by such plain dealing. People who are involved personally in an irregularity are often teased about it by others, but in obscure language which could be innocent to the ignorant listener.

By using in these matters the courtesy, pretence, play-acting and secrecy which they use in most social situations, the North Welsh manage to reconcile their verbal adherence to the chapel codes and their frequent breaches of it in fact, and combine in their lives in a most interesting way an active interest in religion with a variety of other entertainments.

For most people, consistent logic is not the aim of most conversation; conversation is a large part of the raw material from which social relationships are created and the utterance of contradictory opinions and the expression of contradictory moral maxims are reflections of contradictory feelings and behaviour common to human beings everywhere. Different moral laws come into play for different situations and different people; promises are sacred in one social context and 'like pie-crusts, made to be broken' in another social context; religious rules are applied in some traditional situations and forgotten in others.

CHAPTER NINE

COMMUNITY

I n this chapter I shall discuss the bonds that link people of the parish and of its component villages and hamlets together; the organized activities they join in and the informal bonds that unite them; and what qualifications village, parish and district have as the unit which best deserves the name community.

Organizations give shape to a community and the activities they organize give life to a community, but I did not conclude that the role of Llan's organizations was as important socially as that of many informal institutions. Writing about a village on the border between North Wales and England, Frankenberg[1] describes the formal organizations set up to arrange recreational activities which he saw meeting in that village. He found that 'strangers'[2] were chosen to take leading positions in organizations, so that they could be blamed for anything that went wrong. If the community seemed about to be split up by quarrels arising from things going wrong, these 'strangers' were made the scapegoats and the organizations were abandoned. I have tried to see if something similar occurred in Llan.

In Llan foreigners or outsiders took the lead in two of the four recently formed organizations. The president of the Women's

[1] R. Frankenberg, *Village on the Border* (London 1957).

[2] These 'strangers' were very often outsiders, new-comers to the village and/or people considered to be upper-class or intellectual. However, Frankenberg explains 'strangers' is a shifting concept, and a stranger in one context is not a stranger in another. '. . . In nearly every group activity it is possible to recognize someone who has only that activity in common with the other members of the group or is a deviant in some respect from the distinguishing criteria of the group mainly concerned.' One of his examples is of a man who is the chairman of an otherwise all ladies' committee. Nevertheless most of the actual cases of blaming the 'stranger' which he discusses involve a new-comer to the village.

Institute was English and the preceding president and one past secretary had been English. On the two occasions when this Women's Institute chose representatives to send to a London Conference, they chose Englishwomen, in one case the English wife of a Welsh farmer and, in the other case, me. I was the secretary of the youth club, and a Scots lady, likely to be in the parish for only a few years, was the most active helper. The Women's Institute opened in 1958, the youth club in 1959.

The older-established organizations are chapel-based ones such as the Sunday schools, the 'seiatau' or holy societies attached to the two Methodist chapels which meet on weekdays; and the religious organizations, the chapels and church themselves. Sometimes in winter 'little concerts' are held, in Dinas where they are interdenominational and in Carmel where they are run by a committee of the Methodist chapel; and a Christmas party for the children is held in Carmel. Groups of Welshspeaking people, members of the religious congregations, are elected at chapel meetings to arrange these activities. Outside scapegoats are not found to shoulder responsibility for possible disasters.

The coming of the newer organizations, by catering separately for women, young people and those interested in farming, implies the break-up of the chapel's social provision for all members of the family. It reflects a changing situation: a loosening of community bonds in the parish. The social situation in Llan may be coming to resemble that in Frankenberg's village in some respects: the prominence of outsiders in two of the new organizations may mean that the looser community bonds make conflict, even conflict as well covered up as is Llanconflict, less permissible, and therefore make scapegoats necessary.

I do not think that this is the case. Llan is a Welsh-speaking parish; Pentrediwaith seems to be a village in which Welsh is spoken. Llan is firmly embedded in the most Welsh part of Wales and the quarries and factories to which many Llan men travel to work are in this same part of Wales; all the workers are Welsh-speaking and belong to the community of North Wales. Pentrediwaith is on the border and most of its men travel to work either in England or in English-speaking districts where they work with people they would never meet outside the factory. In Llan those permanent residents who do not speak Welsh are quite clearly foreigners, new-comers and outsiders. Their children are taught in Welsh and will, if they stay there, belong to Llan. In one of Pentrediwaith's two infant schools, the children are taught in English although it seems that many of them are of Welsh parentage. The Pentre parish council is described as a stronghold of the Welsh language but the proceedings at its annual general meetings and other public meetings are either entirely in English or bilingual. There are many mixed marriages in Pentre. In Llan there exist five and the children of these five marriages have started speaking Welsh as soon as they started attending school, or earlier. The English partners in these Llan marriages all understand Welsh.

In Llan, then, the language difference makes the insiders and the outsiders immediately recognizable, and the threat of obliteration of the community's identity by English culture, while feared, is not real so long as the Welsh language maintains its strong position. Outsiders are not chosen to play a prominent part in the older organizations and in two of the new ones: the Young Farmers' Club which opened after the war and closed in 1958, and the inter-denominational 'cymdeithas', mainly because they do not attend their meetings. It is difficult to tell whether English people do not go to these meetings because they are held in Welsh or whether they are held in Welsh because English people do not go to them but it seems most likely that meetings of the Young Farmers' Club would have been held in English if any English farmers had attended. Like the youth club and the Women's Institute, it met for a particular reason and to cater for the interests of a particular group. If English people of that group had joined in their meetings the members would have spoken English because, in the limited context of the club, what they had in common was more important than the differences between them. The older chapel-based organizations and the 'cymdeithas' are trying to cater for all age and interest groups – of Welsh people. Whether English people attend or not, meetings are held in Welsh. The 'cymdeithas' is the most interesting of the new organizations and grew up in the following way. Meetings of discussion societies called 'cymdeithasau' used to be held in the two Methodist chapels: the Carmel one still organizes occasional lectures and 'little concerts'; the Dinas one ceased to function in 1954. In the winter of 1958 the minister and one of the deacons of Dinas chapel invited the church congregation, the Baptists and the Carmel chapel to help form a committee and thus started a discussion group in the schoolhouse, open to all and called it a 'cymdeithas'. In its modern form the 'cymdeithas' is like a quiz programme with a slightly religious bias, and those who organize it do so with the conscious intention of preserving typically Welsh institutions and with them Welsh culture. Things have not got so desperate in Llan that English people are called in to save Welsh culture. Llan is not a village on the border and its people can afford to blame each other, though not face to face, and have occasional underground quarrels. Frankenberg writes about recreational activities in Pentrediwaith that they 'provide a medium through which internal village disputes and conflicts find expression. . . . When an activity is abandoned the conflicts within the village are, temporarily at least, suspended at the same time as the activity they have killed. Thus village unity is emphasized and maintained.' In Llan, disputes about parish affairs, such as why the youth club closed down in previous years or what should be done with the money collected between the wars for a playing field, rumble on. At various times, committees have been chosen to sit and decide what should be done about the playing-field money, but the comments by villagers did not subside when the committee was not sitting. Similarly, nothing was healed when an earlier attempt to have a youth club in the church hall failed. The church hall was left empty and unused and the young people had nowhere to go. In these and other disputes Llan people disparage the state of affairs, and when talking to their intimates put the blame at someone's door but not at the door of a particular outsider, stranger or Englishman. They can afford to blame each other because there is more to unite them economically and culturally than there is to unite Pentrediwaith. The operation of the scapegoat principle takes place on a higher level. England and the English are blamed for major ills in rural North Wales generally. England is politically a scapegoat but individual English-speaking people are not used personally as scapegoats.

I do not think, then, that Llan organizations need particular outsiders[1] as scapegoats and I do not think that English people are chosen to lead two of the newer organizations because they are required to act in that role. I think they are chosen for three other reasons. Firstly, just because these organizations are new and unfamiliar, they may provoke unfamiliar snags; letters may have to be written, grants applied for, correspondence may have to be in English (the Women's Institute, for instance, is affiliated to the National Federation of Women's Institutes centred in London). Llan people 'don't know' how to cope with such things; that is, for fear of embarrassment they prefer not to compete, to leave such things as correspondence in English to English people, should any English people be available. Secondly, the newer organizations give scope to those who are seeking prestige on the English ladder. They take an active part themselves and show their friendship to the English by pressing them to take prominent parts.

The third and most important reason why outsiders are chosen to lead two of the newer organizations is the feeling, strongly connected with the idea of keeping face, that it is not 'Welsh' to put yourself forward. When English are present to be put forward, they are put forward. The Welsh system of values is in this respect reminiscent of the American Pueblo tribe called the Zuni who are said to have trouble in finding leaders for just this reason.[2] Welsh leaders are found in the parish council, which is all Welsh-speaking, and in the chapel-based organizations. The footpaths and cemeteries must be maintained. The Christmas Party must be organized; there ought to be a 'little concert'. The workers are known and the work gets done. There is a Welsh way of getting things done: a rather circuitous, slow way. Once English people, and those seeking prestige on the

[1] To simplify comparison I have looked for the more obvious category of outsider or foreigner. Apart from the foreigners I mention, leaders of organized activities in Llan are not 'strangers' or deviants from the group they lead as are some of the leaders in Pentrediwaith, though of course leaders or people very active in organization are bound to have some unusual and outstanding characteristics.

[2] R. Benedict, *Patterns of Culture* (London 1935).

English prestige ladder, join in an activity, it is no longer a really Welsh activity: the Welshness of the Welsh side makes them inevitably lose: to battle to keep control would be to be un-Welsh. So when there are English-speaking participants in the youth club and the Women's Institute, then the English are put into the leading roles, where they are potentially as 'pushing' and as 'bossy' as the Welsh stereotype of the English portrays them to be.

It is difficult for organizations to survive in small villages. The old type of organization, based mainly on the chapel, does not fit in with today's requirments. It grew up in a time when old men dominated society and when the family was a more important social unit than it is today. The chapel 'societies', Sunday schools, parties and concerts were held for all members of the family. The women did the work, the men held the positions, the children learned and obeyed. The North Welsh father of between the wars expected obedience. The much greater respect shown for age in North Wales than in England carries with it inevitably a feeling that young people should be respectful.

The whole climate of opinion in Britain has changed and this change has affected Llan. Young people earn far more than they ever have earned; they are more important in the country as a whole; they form a larger proportion of the population than they used to, and employers, politicians, salesmen and moralizers want to attract their attention. The speed with which social change is taking place puts generations more widely out of touch with each other than they have been before. Young people still go to chapel, are still confirmed in their teens, still sing hymns and address people older than themselves as 'you', but they want independence and their own meeting-place. Similarly, the Women's Institute gives women a chance to follow their own interests, which rarely include theological discussion. The Young Farmers' Club met a need for discussion and education of a type which the chapel could not provide. But the 'particular-interest' organizations find it as hard to survive as does the old type of organization. In a small, sparsely populated parish, there are not enough young farmers, not enough women, not enough teenagers, to provide three workable groups meeting once a week all through the winter.

The chapel people, realizing that the new situation needed a new treatment, began the 'cymdeithas' which was 'chapel' in that it was organized by religious organizations, was open to all ages and sexes to join, was Welsh and had a religious bias, but was modern in the sense that it used some of the methods of modern entertainment to attract young people and women. Posters announced that the 'cymdeithas' was to have a Brains Trust or Twenty Questions. A panel of people faced the rest; there was an open clash of opinions and personalities; local equivalents of Gilbert Harding and Lady Barnett amused the audience and the 'cymdeithas' was a success. Numbers as large, for Llan, as fifty and sixty were attracted and the 'cymdeithas' seems most likely of all the parish organizations to survive.

The difficulty of running organizations in the parish is attributed by some Llan people to a fading of community spirit and here I think it is worth while to discuss which unit best deserves the name community.

I think a place deserving the name community forms or has in the past formed some kind of economic unit, so that a substantial proportion of its inhabitants were economically interdependent. Such a situation encourages families to settle and grow and form the fairly stable population needed for the formation of the criss-crossing ties of kinship which are the raw material of community life. I do not mean to imply that social groups in Llan, whether for economic co-operation or for social functions, are based on kinship as a principle of organization. This is not the case, as I have shown in previous chapters. People are recruited to the community by kinship; they then join in grouping according to age, sex, vicinity and economic interest. Kinship gives continuity to the life of the parish. There is a time-lag between changes in the economic foundation and changes in the social and ceremonial life: it takes some time for that life to grow up and it takes some time for it to die down because it takes some time for families to grow up and learn and to disband and forget. A place that has been an economic unit and a kin-tied community will continue to see itself as a community long after it ceases to be an economic unit, and will therefore be a community. The durability and quality of its community life will depend on such factors as geographical position; the presence or absence of able and enthusiastic people; the distance to work opportunities and whether those opportunities are varied or consist of one workplace employing mainly manual workers; the distance to the nearest cinema; and so on.

Frankenberg writes: 'If a village . . . is a village it undertakes activities which are village activities. All individuals are expected to join in independently of their relations with one another . . . if there are no such activities we have a housing unit and not a village.'

I do not agree. A village, or parish, or town, or district which is an economic unit or has been an economic unit within living memory of its inhabitants is a community with real ties between its members, whether or not it has village, parish, town or district activities; and a suburb of commuters with a dance held in the 'community centre' open to all who live in the suburb cannot be a community in the same sense. There is not enough incentive for the population to remain stable long enough for family ties to grow up: if people could get work in their suburb they might find it worth while to support some overcrowding in order to stay; but this being impossible, sons and daughters of the original commuters will move elsewhere.

Thus although the parish of Llan and the central village of Dinas have ceased to be economic units, although some years pass in which they have no parish or village activities open to all, they are communities and not just housing units.

Most people in Llan celebrate Christmas only in their families. But a few young women of the parish, none of whom would drink in Llan throughout the year, drink with their husbands in the pub at Christmas time. Everyone in Llan does not celebrate Christmas in the pub, no more than everyone celebrates it in chapel. Nor do the celebrations attract two mutually exclusive groups: one to the pub and one to the chapel: some celebrate in both places. Such small overlapping groups, formal and informal, engage in every public activity in Llan. There is no activity in which all individuals do actually join (though they could all join in the 'cymdeithas') not because of rigid class distinctions; not because of powerful religious divisions; but because people's interests and pleasures do crisscross, do not correlate very neatly. The social groups which affect most people's lives most often in Llan are the informal groups in which they usually join with one or more of their kin: neighbourhood groups such as the residents of Pensarn hamlet who might go to the seaside together in the summer; work groups, such as the farmers who lend tools, machinery and labour to one another and may go to an agricultural show together; groups of poachers; groups of young mothers who see each other at clinics or travel together to them; groups of men who play darts together in the pub and might go to the Isle of Man together to see the motor-cycle races, or play football on Christmas Day. These overlapping social groups, mainly informal, spread over three main circles of community: village, parish and district.[1]

A person who lives in the village of Dinas belongs to enough of the groups or takes part in enough of the activities to feel that he belongs to Dinas. He sees his village as a community because he belongs to these groups, because it was an economic unit for many years and because it is the centre of the parish of Llan.

A person who lives in the village of Carmel has a stronger feeling of belonging to Carmel than a Dinas person has to Dinas. Dinas people agreed that if they tried to imagine themselves equipped with a label saying who they were and where they came from, their labels would say 'Welsh – from Llan'; whereas Carmel people's imaginery labels would say 'Welsh – from Carmel'. This is partly because Carmel is still an economic unit: the core of its population is a group of mountain-sheep farmers who depend upon one another to keep their farms going. It is partly because Carmel is geographically isolated; partly because the community life that grew up in Carmel – after 1850 when the quarry opened there – around a nucleus of quarrymen who lived and worked in the village was very rich; and partly because, as a result of the factors already mentioned, more of

[1] Informal social groupings cross parish boundaries and overlap with similar informal groupings all over North Wales whereas formal organizations which meet in the parish are based on parish boundaries. The Llan W.I. is affiliated to a larger organization and sometimes joins with neighbouring W.I.'s or sends delegates to regional conferences, but its membership, the group that meets in Llan, as is general with formal organizations, is limited to people who live in the parish.

the social life in Carmel takes place in organized groups than in informal groups, and therefore the community is more self-consciously a community.

A sense of belonging to the village is the first circle of community spirit. It is much weaker than it was one hundred years ago because the economic independence of the villages is less and therefore the population has not remained stable.

The bulk of people living in Llan do not live in villages and their first loyalty is to the second circle of community spirit: the parish. People living in Dinas, Carmel and the hamlets and scattered farmsteads feel that they belong to the parish of Llan, not mainly because it can sometimes boast an organization open to all Llan inhabitants but because historically it has been their most important economic unit and so had a population about which it is still true to say that most of them are related to each other. To them, too, it is the centre, as is his own parish for every person in the district, of a cultural entity which for its inhabitants has been becoming such an entity over the past century and which is the third level of community spirit: Gwynedd or North West Wales.

The community spirit is elusive to the people involved and they think it much less than it was in their childhood, partly because that spirit has been spread out over a larger grouping than they visualize as suitable or possible for a community in spatial terms. Emigration and immigration have moved the population of North Wales about and most people living in Llan have kin elsewhere in Gwynedd. Of 207 marriages between 1895 and 1959 in which one or both of the partners were living in Llan, in only 60 did the couple settle in Llan. The rest settled, with very few exceptions, in other parts of Gwynedd. Gwynedd has thus become an important unit in the hierarchy of communities: a unit forming some sort of economic unit around the slate quarries. It also has a cultural distinction in its language, but this does not form a boundary, since the rural areas in which Welsh is spoken extend south into Cardiganshire and Carmarthenshire and east into parts of Denbigh and Montgomeryshire.

I have said that Gwynedd is an important unit in the hierarchy of communities and it is a community in a sense. Before the industrial revolution affected North Wales, Llan, like other rural parishes in the district, was a subsistence farming community with natural boundaries of bare mountain and wide river separating it from similar communities. When new work opportunities on roads, railways, ports and in the quarries caused the pattern of living to spread over those natural boundaries, the markets and hiring fairs, to which people travelled from far and wide, became more important and these county and district events are still important social events. Fairs and the eisteddfodau are the formal ceremonials of this widest community: overlapping groups of poachers are the informal means by which its male members are joined in a proud Welsh, anti-English feeling of community.

As transport facilities improve and 'village economies' break down, a tendency may be found in many places for people to transfer much of their allegiance from the village to a wider unit. In rural North Wales, many factors encourage this transference. If a man from Merioneth joins the British armed forces and meets another man who speaks the dialect of Welsh spoken in North West Wales, there is a very good chance that he will know somebody of whom the other man has at least heard, before he went into the forces. Gwynedd has a small population as well as having a cultural distinction in its language.

CHAPTER TEN

CHANGE

AFTER centuries in which Wales was virtually untouched by England's conquest, it was hit by the Industrial Revolution in the nineteenth century. The mineral products of South Wales were plentiful and valuable and in the course of its industrialization that part of Wales was anglicized. North Wales was known to have cheap labour and plentiful water power and was thought to be rich in minerals and so roads were opened; copper was mined in Anglesey; coal was mined in Flint; slate was quarried in Caernarvon and Merioneth. But 'local seams were thin and broken; the veins of ore petered out or were submerged; water power fell out of fashion. The harbours kept silting up and the districts richest in natural products often proved the poorest in natural outlets and the most intractable to transport . . . Capital withdrew to regions . . . richer in coal, and with better harbours. These factors brought the industrial revolution in North Wales to an untimely close, at a time when, in the richer coalfield of the south (which had started almost level in the race) the real industrial revolution was just beginning.'[1] By 1850 nothing but slate was left. The success of the slate quarries kept ports open, brought roads and railways, and the population of North Wales began to concentrate on ports and slate towns, and increased. But by 1894 the slate industry, too, had begun to decline as a result of foreign competition and competition from the tile industry, and it never fully recovered after the 1914–18 war. The economic forces which had stirred North Wales up, then left it flat. The population first declined and then, with the help of retired English people moving to settle on the coast, recovered but did not increase above its old peak. North Wales was not left as it had

[1] A. H. Dodd, *Industrial Revolution in North Wales* (Cardiff 1958).

been before the upheaval. Firstly, the whole process, and especially the improved transport facilities, had brought North Wales into close contact with England and this contact was increased with the coming of films, radio and television. Secondly, the dislocation in people's lives, and particularly that caused by emigration and unemployment which followed the decline of the slate industry, and the affluence of the English quarry-owners and landlords compared to the extreme poverty of the farmers between the wars, combined to give North Welsh people a strong sense of injustice having been committed against them. Thirdly, the attempt made in the nineteenth century to impose English speech on the Welsh-speaking population, and the penetration of North Wales by the British Civil Service, which put the 'conquest' finally into effect; combined with the sense of injustice mentioned above to make North Welsh people conscious of themselves as a group of Welsh-speaking people left in Wales: weakened in number by emigration and at bay before the threat of the English language.

I shall discuss in this chapter, first what effect these factors – nearness to England, sense of economic injustice, and the growth of nationalism – have had on Welsh culture as it survived after the changes brought and left by the Industrial Revolution; secondly, some suggestions that have been made for the future preservation of that culture; and thirdly, other agents of change.

The threat to Welsh culture may be measured by its two most obvious pointers: population and language. If these decline, Welsh culture could hardly survive. The language carries the tradition and the people carry the language. The same jokes could not be told in English; the peculiar flavour of the bargaining game would not exist if it were played in English; and if the population declined further the main carriers of the language would be the groups of exiles spread from London to Patagonia, whose versions of the Welsh way of life must be various and coloured by their new locality. By the first of these pointers, population, Welsh culture is not holding its own, as will be seen from Appendix 1.

When discussing the Welsh language, some writers take such a long period that the figures show the Welsh language to be flourishing. Thus R. T. Jenkins writes: 'Beyond any doubt there are, in absolute numbers, far more people speaking Welsh today than at any previous stage in our long history – the entire population of Wales 200 years ago was not half as numerous as is the Welsh-speaking fraction of it today.'[1]

In this century, the decline in the proportion of the population speaking Welsh has been continuous, even in the very Welsh county of Merioneth.

Percentage of population over 3 speaking Welsh at each decennial census since 1901.

	Wales and Monmouth			Merionethshire		
	Welsh only	English and Welsh	Total Welsh speakers	Welsh only	English and Welsh	Total Welsh speakers
1901	15·1	34·8	49·9	50·6	43·1	93·7
1911	8·5	35·0	43·5	36·7	53·6	90·3
1921	6·3	30·8	37·1	29·7	52·4	82·1
1931	4·0	32·8	36·8	22·1	64·0	86·1
1951	1·7	27·2	28·9	9·2	66·2	75·4

Thus if the long time-span is looked at, by the second pointer of language, the Welsh culture is holding its own. But the undeniable and steady trend of this century gives no cause for optimism. And other, less obvious signs point in the same direction.

In the graphs made to illustrate the trends discussed in this book, the curves for North Wales and the curves for England and Wales as a whole begin far apart and, as they approach the present day, come closer together. Whatever in Welsh culture made for relatively high rates of illegitimacy, late average age at marriage, and so on, those elements are losing their effect.

Some forces are working for, others against, the preservation of Welsh culture. The first part of the legacy left from the Industrial Revolution, mentioned above, closer contact with England, works against it. In a similar way, closer contact between the various parts of the world makes them less diverse.

[1] R. T. Jenkins, *The Development of Nationalism in Wales. Sociological Review*, 1935.

The second and third parts of the legacy left by the Industrial Revolution act in favour of Welsh culture. The sense of injustice, and nationalism, have fed each other and made North Welsh people consciously proud of their language and made many of them actively fight against the threat of further emigration, and dilution of the culture.

There are many other things that most North Welsh people want more than they want their country to remain Welsh. But the fact that they share this desire with each other makes them alike and makes them still different from their English-speaking neighbours.

There is a top and official side to the battle to retain Welsh culture which I have hardly touched on for two reasons. Firstly, because it is the vocal side which has been publicized: as when the Board of the BBC Welsh Region objected to the appointment of a non-Welsh-speaking member; or when Welsh members of the Parliamentary Labour Party campaign for special treatment of Welsh affairs. Secondly, because I am ill-informed about that top and official side to the battle. It seems remote from the daily happenings in the countryside. When Lord Raglan pronounced that only illiterates[1] spoke Welsh, the outcry resounded in Llan's pub, but generally the 'preserve

[1] 'Welsh is the language of the illiterate Welsh, English of the literate Welsh . . . Most of the speakers of Welsh are, as I have said, illiterate or semi-literate, but there are a few thousand people who have learnt to speak the literary language, and who make a regular cult of it. These may be divided into three classes, which though they overlap, may be considered separately. First come the scholars, those who make a study of the old Welsh literature. Those of them who . . . publish their results in English, perform a very valuable function, but those who publish in Welsh merely cut themselves off from the international fellowship of scholars.

'The second class consists of those who hope, by their knowledge of Welsh, to obtain preference for posts for which they are otherwise ill qualified. There are, of course, certain posts for which a knowledge of Welsh is essential, but they are few, for the number of Welsh people who have not a working knowledge of English is small. Thirdly come the nationalists, who, unless they are much maligned, use it largely to stir up hatred of England among the more ignorant Welsh.

'The Welsh language is thus used for at least three undesirable purposes, to conceal the results of scholarship, to try to lower the standards of official competence and, worst of all, to create enmity where none existed.'

Lord Raglan. Article in *Wales*, October 1958. Tudor Press Ltd.

Welsh' campaign which gets into the newspapers is not closely related to the partisan warfare I observed.

In the battle to retain their culture, Llan people are not organized; they do not fight openly on a clear platform; they are not agreed upon a policy: for tourism or against tourism, for a national park or against a national park. They are individuals, proud if the beauty of their home has made it a national park but needy enough to put up a bed-and-breakfast sign or erect a corrugated iron shed and sell teas and iced 'lollies' in that national park if they can manage to. They will be hospitable to tourists as individuals, but resent them in bulk as an invasion and a traffic problem. They do not earn their living by waging the battle but their lives are coloured always by their attachment to their Welshness and a reluctance to surrender it. All their resentments as working-class people against the ruling class; as country people against the towns; as ordinary people against powerful officials, are poured into the Welsh-versus-English mould and give a strength to the battle which it would not otherwise possess.

The Welsh way of life is really threatened, and Welsh people react to the threat in subtle ways. The successful woman who lives in a big house, sits on many committees, is very active politically and 'does good' is scorned: she speaks English to her children and is at the bottom of the Welsh prestige ladder.

The 'matey' Englishman who knows just what to do about a broken car or how to make money is – agreed with; and never knows the partisan lifemanship that is practised on him. That same 'pretending not to know' softens the relations between the Welsh people themselves and enables them to live together with few breaches of neighbourliness.

The officials, bailiffs and policemen are watched and reported on by the grapevine – and foiled annually in the poaching season, and in other ways.

So with their own weapons, their own medals, their own heroes, their own traitors, the Welsh-speaking people of rural North Wales defend their Welshness and pursue the class struggle.

Their actions run parallel and on a different level to the remedies suggested on the top and official level. These remedies include improved housing in the villages; increased grants for the arts; training facilities for young people; facilities for sports and entertainment. However, the main remedy suggested, and the one to which all others seem subsidiary, is that of bringing industry into the area, and this is of tremendous interest to the North Welsh people themselves. Most people say that Welsh culture cannot survive without industry; without a better choice of jobs and thus an incentive to the population not to leave; but there are others who say that industry will kill Welsh culture. This remedy could prove destructive in the following way. The natural growth of a population takes place slowly: the number of unemployed at any one time in a sparsely populated rural area such as North Wales is small. Although the percentage of the population which is unemployed is higher than in most other parts of England and Wales, the population is meagre: much emigration has taken place, and therefore the number of unemployed people at any one time is very small. The chances are high that any big new industry that opens in North Wales will be able to offer high enough wages and good enough conditions (especially travelling facilities) to attract most of the unemployed men from a very wide area. But if it is a big concern, the total of unemployed men, even in that wide area, will not be nearly enough to supply its needs for a labour force. The firms that can make the most substantial contribution to the economy of North Wales, therefore, bring what could be the worst threat to the culture of North Wales in the form of a large influx of English labour.

Llan has been affected by two such industries: an atomic power station and an electricity storage scheme; both having opened within fifteen miles of the parish in the years during which this study was made. Buses carry workers to these two sites from distances of fifty miles. There were 800 unemployed in the district when the atomic power station came, but although 792 of 1505 men they employ[1] are local men, there are still almost as many men unemployed in the district. The work on the sites is such that the unskilled must do heavy work, in the open. Old men or men who are not very fit cannot, therefore, be employed. For young strong men there is some competition in

[1] This was written in February 1961.

North Wales, in spite of the unemployment figures, which as I have said above are large proportionately in relation to the rest of England and Wales but not large absolutely. Some small slate quarries have closed down since the power station and the storage scheme began, mainly through lack of labour. The quarrymen may not have gone to work on the sites; they may have gone to fill jobs left open by men who did go. Danger from silicosis makes work in the quarries very unpopular so that alternative employment may not end unemployment in the district but act at the expense of the quarries. This is not to suggest that the unemployed people are unemployable; the older and not very strong men could be usefully employed in other kinds of industry.

The coming of industry does not necessarily mean the end of the unemployment problem and in the case of the power station and the storage scheme it certainly has not done so, and will not have done so in the long run, as when the constructions are finished only 400 men will be employed on the power station, and fewer on the storage scheme. Indirectly, however, the schemes have affected the employment situation favourably. The often exaggerated reports of the high wages that can be earned on the schemes have made farm-workers and general labourers elsewhere stiffen slightly in their relations with their employers. The existence of alternative work makes all workers more valuable.

Though most effects of the schemes will be temporary, it is worth inquiring who exactly goes to work on the schemes. What financial gains are being made by the district and what effects will the invasion of outsiders have on the local culture?

Many firms came to the district with contracts to do certain parts of the work on the two schemes, and there were many subsidiary constructions. The harbour of a small port has been deepened to allow large machinery to be brought by sea, and the roads from the harbour to the power station have been widened and straightened.

On one section of the road, two gangs composed of thirty-one local men and eight foreigners were employed. Of the eight foreigners, one had been living in the district for a while and was employed as a labourer like the Welshmen; the other seven were imported either by the road-improvement firm or by other firms connected with the two main schemes. The seven imported men were the engineer, the agent, the foreman, two gangers and the driver of the steam-roller. Only two of the four gangers were Welsh. Figures from the main contractors show that of the 713 imported men on the power station, the great majority are engineers, welders, boiler-makers, carpenters and other skilled men. Carpenters were so scarce that a labour manager was sent to Ireland to look for them. Whilst many Welsh people are prepared to admit that there are not sufficient trained Welshmen to supply engineers, agents and craftsmen for the new constructions, other have prominent in their minds the fact that the top jobs go to the English.[1] They know there are not enough Welsh engineers and carpenters but they feel there are many Welshmen who could be gangers, foremen and steam-roller drivers. The practice of employing Englishmen as supervisors has a long history and in 1847 a Government Commissioner wrote: 'In the works the Welsh workman never finds his way into the office. He never becomes either clerk or agent.'[2]

On the road-improvement site, of the Welshmen, more than half were married. They were not men who had been unemployed for a long time before the road improvement began. Nor had most of them left steady jobs to do that work. They were in the main the particularly unstable section of a working population which as a whole is never very stable. They were easygoing and confident; happy to earn high wages for a time, ready to leave a job quickly if they disliked it, and feeling that a small chance of further work at the end of the present plenty of jobs, and the certainty of the dole, were sufficient insurance against insecurity. The bulk of employees in the factory and quarries, and those working on the roads for the County Council, were not tempted by the higher money offered on the schemes because of the insecurity and only three men in Llan have gone to work on the new schemes.

Nor has Llan been affected by the search for accommodation for the imported men. The higher grades buy or rent houses or

[1] By English they mean English, Irish or Scottish.

[2] Report of Commissioners for Inquiry into the State of Education in Wales, 1847.

live on a small housing estate which has been built for some of the power-station staff. Of the other imported workers, 505 of them live in a camp and 120 live in lodgings and pay quite high rates for board and lodging. Many go back to England for the week-ends. Llan is not near or convenient enough to the sites for outsiders to live there and so only two Llan houses have had lodgers, and those only for a brief time.

Whilst there is extra custom in all the pubs and shops of the area, and the value of houses has gone up; new shops have not sprouted up and on the surface North Wales has not become noticeably richer as a result of the schemes: the effect has been general and slight.

The effect of the schemes on Welsh culture is difficult to gauge partly because it is early to try to do so, and partly because the sites are ten and fifteen miles from Llan and the impact is not great in that parish.

The village nearest to the atomic power stations is a tiny village whose farms support about half the population. Most of the other men work in the quarry. During the recent world war, an army camp was located near by and provided some work for the village, particularly for the women, and now the atomic power station has taken the place of the army camp. Through all these changes, with all these outside influences, the village has appeared to remain as strong a Welsh community as, for instance, the Carmel of Llan parish, and so far it is as intensely Welsh-speaking as the most untouched Welsh village.

In a pub midway between Llan and the power station, a group of workers from Liverpool were so impressed by the singing, and by the close feeling of the group that met there to sing, that they learned the Welsh hymns. They also learnt enough Welsh words to be able to express respect for the elderly leader of the singing group, without whose nod no song could start with any hope of success.

Elsewhere, inhabitants have complained of drunkenness among the foreign workers.

Unlike the opening of the South Welsh coalfields, the schemes are not so lasting in their disturbance as to affect permanently the Welsh way of life in rural North Wales.

If industry on a small scale were established permanently in various places over North Wales, the extra employment would give incentive to people to stay rather than to emigrate. Such action would help the survival of Welsh culture. The present large-scale but short-term industries have little direct effect on Welsh culture. The presence of a large number of foreign workmen puts the local people on their guard; the unemployment situation is relieved for a time, over a wide area; sections of the population which do not usually prosper have made good wages and will be dissatisfied with the probable reduction when the schemes are over. Perhaps the most important effect of the industries discussed is that they have stimulated improved transport facilities: a harbour has been deepened, roads have been widened. If small permanent industries can be persuaded to come to North Wales, one of the arguments which will bring them will be the improved communications which will reduce their costs.

I have been discussing remedies that have been proposed to save Welsh culture from decline. I conclude this chapter by pointing out what I believe are the two main agents of change which are causing encroachment on that culture and will do so in the future: the increased nearness to England mentioned earlier in this chapter; and the economic changes which followed the Second World War. There are two key groups which are affected by these factors: young people and farmers.

It is easy for any young person to go to London, Birmingham or abroad now, in the police force or merchant navy, as a nurse, as a Civil Servant, working in a shop or in an office. Films, radio and television bring the world of big towns near, familiar and unfrightening. If the young people go and do not come back they will affect adversely both of the main pointers to the health of the culture: population and language, since the Welsh language must have young people to carry it if it is to survive. Language is being undermined also in a more direct way. Even those young people who have a strong affection and loyalty for Wales and all things Welsh find much of their pleasure and entertainment, as well as their education, comes to them in the medium of English; they write to their absent friends in English and say they find it easier to write in English though they prefer to talk in Welsh. If young people feel no incentive to continue using Welsh, the fact that Welsh is the first language in the schools will not make them use it. If in particular the economic incentive to give English first place continues high, the best-paid jobs going to the people who speak English well, then even a Welsh Government in Wales, encouraging the Welsh language by every possible means, could not save the Welsh language. The examples of Ireland in this century and North Wales (where every effort was made to stamp out the Welsh language in the schools and all failed) in the last century are sufficiently similar to the present situation in Wales to show this. The main ground for optimism for the Welsh language is the similar plight facing other languages. As the world shrinks the need for a world language becomes pressing. Anglo-American or some form of the English language seems most likely to take on the role. But the Arabic, French, German, Hindu, Russian and other major languages with rich literatures will not accept oblivion and, if things happen quickly enough, the Welsh language will find itself in good company in its fight for self-preservation.

Since the Second World War, farmers in Llan have become relatively wealthy. They are a numerous section of the working population and until now they have lived in the same style as other manual workers in Llan. If, as seems very likely, their prosperity makes them less dependent upon each other and removes them socially from their neighbours, they will do more than any influx of outsiders could do to break up the Welsh way of life and the solidarity of Welsh-speaking people and undermine the culture. Firstly, because the Welsh-speaking people cannot afford to lose a part of their strength in their struggle to keep their Welshness, they need to be unified. Secondly, because part of the Welsh system of values is the likeness of the way of life and standard of life of everyone holding those values. It is hard to imagine the Welsh culture surviving after the growth of a middle class. It grew up in scattered farmsteads and was nourished in 'merry nights', at individual farms at shearing parties and by the piety of the farmers. It transplanted strongly to the quarries, but continues to need the farms as an important part of its home.

The farmers' feelings are strongly engaged in trying to keep the old life going. But their economic position inclines them and inclines their children still more to become more and more like English farmers. These children, in big modern cars, will take holidays, will improve their houses, and will send their children to agricultural colleges. Despite themselves, the farmers are the group inside the local system which welcomes attacks from the outside on the system.

In this book I have tried to show that into the mould of anti-English feeling in North Wales go country people's antagonism towards town people; ordinary people's antagonism towards officials; and working-class people's antagonism towards those with power over them. It follows that part of the strength of these people's Welshness comes from the fact that it includes their sense of being country people; their sense of being ordinary people; their sense of being working people. So that even if the Welsh language were to fall into disuse completely; the Welsh population to decline still further, and the farmers to become 'middle-class'; and the Welsh culture were to vanish as a result of these changes: a consciousness of being Welsh as opposed to English will remain so long as young people in North Wales continue to be country people, ordinary people and working people.

CONCLUSION

In this study I have not attempted to describe or survey life in the parish of Llan. I have given only as much background as seemed essential for an understanding of the discussion of the paradoxes I had noticed; and to enable some comparison to be made between Llan and the other Welsh country parishes which have been described by social anthropologists, geographers and sociologists.

In looking closer at the lack of class distinctions in the society, and in particular the attitude of Llan people towards white-collared workers and the number of them who were not 'climbing' socially, and at the attitude of Llan people towards officials and their participation in poaching in particular, I found it was necessary to invoke the feeling that Welsh-speaking people have towards England, towards English people and towards anglicized Welsh people. A description of this feeling served two purposes. It made the paradoxes less mysterious to me, and it introduced – as an almost necessary concomitant of the anti-English feeling – a feeling of pride in being Welsh which was shared by Llan people. What it means to be Welsh I have tried to see from an outsider's point of view, and an understanding of Welsh values was the key to an understanding of the third paradox I had noted: which is how Llan people reconcile their public adherence to the chapel's code with their actual permissiveness in sexual matters.

APPENDIX 1 : Population at each decennial census 1801–1961

Year	Merioneth Population	Merioneth Intercensal percentage increase or decrease per annum	Gwynedd[1] Population	Gwynedd[1] Intercensal percentage increase or decrease per annum	England & Wales Population	England & Wales Intercensal percentage increase or decrease per annum	Wales Population	Wales Intercensal percentage increase or decrease per annum
1801	29,506		104,833		8,893,000			
1811	30,854	+0·46	117,554	+1·21	10,164,000	+1·32		
1821	34,382	+1·14	137,544	+1·70	12,000,000	+1·67	794,000	
1831	35,315	+0·27	150,458	+0·94	13,897,000	+1·48	904,000	+1·38
1841	39,322	+1·14	171,316	+1·39	15,914,000	+1·36	1,046,000	+1·57
1851	38,843	−0·13	185,040	+0·80	17,928,000	+1·22	1,163,000	+1·11
1861	38,963	+0·03	189,266	+0·23	20,066,000	+1·13	1,286,000	+1·06
1871	46,598	+1·96	203,920	+0·77	22,712,000	+1·25	1,413,000	+0·99
1881	52,038	+1·12	222,803	+0·93	25,974,000	+1·35	1,572,000	+1·13
1891	48,859	−0·61	217,843	−0·22	29,003,000	+1·11	1,771,000	+1·27
1901	48,852	−0·00	222,939	+0·23	32,528,000	+1·16	2,019,000	+1·40
1911	45,565	−0·67	219,081	−0·17	36,070,000	+1·04	2,421,000	+2·00
1921	45,087	−0·11	225,014	+0·27	37,887,000	+0·48	2,656,000	+0·97
1931	43,201	−0·42	213,059	−0·52	39,952,000	+0·54	2,593,000	−0·24
1941	No census							
1951	41,465	−0·20	216,265	+0·15	43,758,000	+0·48	2,599,000	+0·00
1961	39,007	−0·59	211,901	−0·20	46,071,000	+0·51	2,641,000	+0·16

[1] Gwynedd – Merionethshire, Anglesey and Caernarvonshire.

A reduction in population from one census to the next, as has occurred continuously in Merionethshire since 1891, is a most clear and dramatic indicator of population decline and therefore of movement away from the area. However, the small increases in the three counties Merionethshire, Anglesey and Caernarvonshire together (Gwynedd), when compared with the level of national increase (vide Colum 7) can also be taken as a reliable indicator of the same phenomena. The fact that Gwynedd population figures do not increase with the figures for England and Wales shows that Gwynedd people are still emigrating; and therefore the population of Gwynedd is declining relatively.

APPENDIX 2

Some information on Llan farms changing hands from about 1870 to 1959

1st farm : 1876 Ellis
1892 Owen
1919 Williams
1955 Roberts

2nd farm : 1892 Williams
1910 Griffiths
1932 Evans

3rd farm : 1892 Griffiths
1912 Thomas
1950 Roberts
1956 Roberts

4th farm : 1876 Williams
1892 Evans ⎫
1907 Evans ⎬
1930 Evans ⎭

5th farm : 1892 Williams ⎫
1899 Williams ⎬
1922 Williams ⎭
1936 Davies
1946 Jones
1954 Roberts

6th farm : 1876 Griffiths ⎫
1892 Griffiths ⎭
1921 Williams ⎫
1944 Williams ⎭

7th farm : 1872 Jones
1882 Roberts
1892 Thomas
1902 Williams
1940 Williams

8th farm : 1892 Williams
1907 Thomas
1914 Owen
1938 Richards

9th farm : 1883 Jones ⎫
1892 Jones ⎭
1910 Roberts
1929 Jones
1940 Elias
1942 Lewis

10th farm : 1890 Evans
1906 Davies
1931 Evans
1952 Jones

11th farm : 1876 Jones ⎫
1884 Jones ⎭
1892 Griffiths
1920 Griffiths ⎫
1942 Griffiths ⎭

12th farm : 1892 Roberts
1934 Roberts
1936 Williams
1940 Jones
1950 Jones
1952 Griffiths

13th farm : 1882 Jones ⎫
1884 Jones ⎭
1887 Buckley
1896 Williams ⎫
1930 Williams ⎭

14th farm : 1870 Williams
1876 Roberts ⎫
1892 Roberts ⎬
1936 Roberts ⎭

15th farm : 1876 Jones
1892 Jones
1915 Pritchard ⎫
1919 Pritchard ⎭
1953 Williams

144

16th farm: 1876 Evans
1889 Evans
1937 Owen

17th farm: 1867 Roberts ⎫
1878 Roberts ⎭
1898 Owen
1911 Roberts
1936 Williams
1944 Richards
1946 Jones
1954 Williams

18th farm: 1892 Roberts
1908 Williams
1930 Jones
1941 Pierce

19th farm: 1865 Griffiths ⎫
1906 Griffiths ⎭
1919 Evans
1940 Pugh

20th farm: 1876 Lloyd ⎫
1896 (Hughes) ⎬
1913 Jones ⎭
1922 Jones ⎫
1940 Jones ⎭

21st farm: 1869 Williams ⎫
1905 Williams ⎭
1916 Jones ⎫
1932 Jones ⎭
1933 Evans
1941 Pugh

22nd farm: 1875 Williams
1876 Roberts
1923 Griffiths ⎫
1924 Griffiths ⎭

1926 Edwards
1973 Jones

Land only: 1938 Pierce &
Jones shared.
Land only: 1940 Jones &
Jones shared.
1949 Williams

23rd farm: 1873 Jones
1916 Parry
1920 Evans ⎫
1926 Evans ⎭

24th farm: 1876 Williams
1909 Crompton
1925 Williams ⎫
1944 Williams ⎭

25th farm: 1934 Pierce
1938 Jones
1942 Ll. Pierce

26th farm: 1882 Isaac
1883 Jones
1899 Roberts
1909 Evans
1926 Jones
1930 Evans
1936 Jones
1951 Williams ⎫
1955 Williams ⎭

27th farm: 1883 Jones ⎫
1928 Jones ⎭
1934 Pierce
1938 Jones
1942 Pierce
1948 Hart

This list is not exhaustive; there were more farms, and on several of the farms more holders than are listed. Each date and accompanying name signifies that, at that time, the holding was being farmed by a different person from the man who was farming it on the date previously mentioned. Changes did not necessarily take place on the dates given. Bracketed names indicate that the holders of those names are kin. In the case of the 20th farm two kinsmen, Lloyd and Jones, are separated by a non-kinsman who intervened.

APPENDIX 3

Children leaving Grammar School in 1937 without taking General Schools Certificate between ages 14–16

England & Wales	Wales	Anglesey	Caernarvon	Merioneth
21%	28%	24%	34%	26%

Secondary Schools on Grant List. Statistics of pupils who left during school year 1936–7. Board of Education. England and Wales. Ref. List 62.

These are the only figures available by which comparisons may be made between different parts of England and Wales for early school leavers and the situation may well be different since the 1944 Education Act.

BIBLIOGRAPHY

OF WORKS TO WHICH REFERENCE HAS BEEN MADE
OR FROM WHICH QUOTATIONS HAVE BEEN TAKEN

On Wales and Welsh History

Giraldus Cambrensis. *Itinerary Through Wales.* Ed. W. Ll.
Williams. J. M. Dent & Sons Ltd. Everyman ed. 1935.

Dodd, A. H. *Industrial Revolution in North Wales.* University of
Wales Press. Cardiff 1958.

Firbank, T. *I Bought A Mountain.* London 1940.

Frankenberg, R. *Village on the Border.* Cohen and West. London
1957.

Hyde Hall, E. *A Description of Caernarvonshire 1809–1811.* Ed.
E. Gwynne-Jones. Caernarvon Historical Society. Record
Series No. 2. Caern. 1952.

Jarman, A. O. H. *The Historical Basis of Welsh Nationalism.* Wade
Evans. Cardiff 1950.

Jenkins, D., & others. *Welsh Rural Communities.* Ed. E. Davies and
A. D. Rees. Univ. of Wales Press. Cardiff 1960.

Jenkins, R. T. *The Development of Nationalism in Wales. Sociological
Review.* 1935.

Jones, S., & Smith, G. P. *Employment and Unemployment in N. W.
Wales.* Bangor 1960.

Owen, N. *Caernarvonshire, a Sketch of its History, Antiquity, Mountains and Productions.* J. Debrett. London 1792.

Owen, R. *Hanes Methodistiaeth Gorllewin Meirionydd.*

Raglan, Lord. Article in *Wales.* Tudor Press Ltd. October 1958.

Rees, A. D. *Life in a Welsh Countryside.* University of Wales Press.
Cardiff 1950.

Williams, D. A. *A History of Modern Wales.* John Murray Ltd.
London 1950.

Bibliography

General Works

Benedict, R. *Patterns of Culture*. London 1935.

Colson, E. *The Makah Indians*. Manchester University Press. Manchester 1958.

Denman and Stewart, *Farm Rents*. London 1959.

Directory of Homes and Hostels for the Care of Unmarried Mothers and Illegitimate Children. National Council for the Unmarried Mother and her Child. 1956 ed. with 1959 amendments.

Evans-Pritchard, E. E. *Witchcraft, Oracles and Magic among the Azande*. Clarendon Press. Oxford 1937.

Hoggart, R. *The Uses of Literacy*. Chatto & Windus Ltd. London 1957.

Hobhouse, C. T., Wheeler, G. C. and Ginsberg, M. *The Material Culture and Social Institutions of the Simpler Peoples*. London 1915.

Murdock, G. P. *Social Structure*. New York 1949.

Pitt-Rivers, J. A. L. F. *The People of the Sierra*. London 1954.

Richards, A. I. *Land, Labour & Diet in Northern Rhodesia*. London, 1939.

Williams, W. M. *Sociology of an English Village*. London 1956.

Wimperis, V. *The Unmarried Mother and her Child*. London 1960.

Young, M. *The Chipped White Cups of Dover*. Unit 2. Distributed by Observer Ltd.

Government Reports, Commissions and Pamphlets

Report of Commissioners of Inquiry into the State of Education in Wales 1847.

Report of Royal Commission on Labour 1891–4.

Report of Royal Commission on Land in Wales and Monmouthshire 1896.

Sir Alfred Mond. Report of the Land Inquiry Committee. Rural. London 1914. Hodder and Stoughton Ltd.

The Place of Welsh and English in the Schools of Wales. Central Advisory Council for Education (Wales) Report.

Welsh Department. Ministry of Education's pamphlet No. 2 on Education in Wales 1847–1947.

Registrar-General's Statistical Review of England and Wales. 1950. Part II Civil.

Commissioner of Inland Revenue Annual Returns. Survey of Incomes. 1954–55.

Report of the Welsh National Serviceman Committee. 3rd Memorandum of the Council for Wales and Monmouthshire 1957.

INDEX

Age differences, 9–10, 35–36, 124, and the youth club, 94

Agriculture, 1; *see also* Farmers, Farming, Farms

Anglicization of gentry, 23, 30, 53, 93, of Welsh people, 30–31, 39, 44, 47

Area to which book refers, 1

Bargaining, 60, 115

Benedict, R., 123n

Borrowing circles, 62–67

'Buchedd A' and 'Buchedd B', 11–12, 100, 114

Cambrensis, G., 18

Change, 124, 130–42
in diet, 18

Chapel, 12, 90–100, 112–14, 120, 122, 124, 126
and illegitimacy, 101–4
and social divisions, 76, 93
as unifying symbol for Welsh, 76, 96–100
attendances, 99
influence of, xv, 37, 101–4

Christmas, 126

Church, 90–95
and social divisions, 76, 93, 96
and the youth club, 94

Class, 23, 30–31, 44
antagonisms, 39, 70, 74, 82, 134, 141
distinctions among Welsh-speakers, lack of, xiv, 5, 73

middle, 140

Climbers, 25

Colson, E., 115 n.

Community, xvii, 6, 12, 53, 119–20, 125–9
Llan man's mental picture of his, 6–7, 10–11
parish as, 128
North West Wales as, 128–9
village as, 127–8

Conscientious objection, 73 n.

Conservative party, 24, 53

Contraception, 105

Council houses, 37, 38

Country versus town, 39, 74, 134, 141

Courting, 7, 106, 111, 112
in bed, 106

Courts, 34, 85, 86

Credit, 16

'Cymdeithas', 121–2, 125, 126

'Cynefin', 55–56

Date to which figures refer, xvii

Davies, E., and Rees, A. D., 114

Denman and Stewart, 61

Diet, 17–19

Disputes, 85–89, 94, 95, 122

Divorce, 117

Dodd, A. H., 130

'Early leavers', 79, 146

Economic, function of poaching, 73–74
life, 15

Economic, *Contd*
  unit, Llan as, 125–6
    North West Wales as, 128
Economy, effect on community
    of, 125–8
  of North Wales, 135
Education, 12, 77–79, 83, 146
Eisteddfodau (singular eistedd-
    fod), 78, 97, 100
Emigration, 128, 131, 135
England, closer contact with, 132
English intellectuals, 11, 24, 25–
    29
English language, 33–35, 131
English people, xix, 2
  as imported labour in Wales,
    135
  as 'knowalls', 115–17, 134
  attitudes of to Welsh language,
    35
  attitudes of Welsh-speaking
    people to, xiv, 4, 22–23, 28–
    29, 47–48, 53, 122–3, 142
  who have married local in-
    habitants, xix
Evans-Pritchard, E. E., xi

Families, xiii, 112, 124
  farm, 66
Farm Implements, sharing of,
    62 ; *see also* Borrowing circles
Farmers, 5–6, 12, 27, 32, 49–68,
    80, 108
  and subsidies and grants, 57,
    59, 60, 81
  disputes between, 87–89
  economic position of, 140
  origin of, 49–50
Farmers' children, 141
Farmers' daughters, 53, 66
Farmers' sons, 49, 52, 53, 54, 66
Farming, 49–68
  as a way of life, 6, 53

Farms, 2, 144–5
  acquisition of, 50–52
  economics of, in Llan, 61
  grants to, 57, 60
  labour force on, 54, 68
  lowland, 54, 58–60
  mountain, 55–58
  size of, 51–52
Farmworker, 50–51, 136
Firbank, T., 15
Frankenberg, R., 23, 119, 126
Frankenberg's village, compari-
    son of with Llan, 120–3

Gift Exchange, 70
'Good things', 107

Hiring Fairs, 10, 99, 100
Hoggart, R., 19, 84
Holidays, 6, 25
Hyde Hall, E., 18, 106 n.

Illegitimacy, xv, 87, 91, 101–18,
    132
Illiteracy, 13, 133
Immigration, 128
Income, of Welsh people, 21
  of landlords, 23
Industrial Revolution, 130–1
Industry, 4, 135–6, 139

Jarman, A.O.H., 30
Jenkins, D., 11, 92 n.
Jenkins, R.T., 132
Jones, S., and Smith, G. P., 21 n.

Kinship, xv, 46, 62, 66, 117, 125

Labour Party, 24, 53, 99
Landlords, 5, 23–25, 26, 30, 82
Law, 48, 80, 85–89, 111
Liberal Party, 99

Manual workers, xvii, 32
Marriage, 87, 104, 106–7, 128
 age at, 87, 108, 110–11, 132
 attractiveness of ideal of, 110–11
 'forced', 106, 108, 111
 of farmers and farmers' children, 53
Method followed, xiii–xiv, 142
Motivation, 69–70, 72–73, 74–76
 and explanation, xvi

Naming, 7–9
National Assistance Board, 84
National Health Service, 77
Nationalism, 131, 133
 in its religious form, 98
 top and official, 133, 134; *see also* Welsh Nationalist Party
Nonconformist Revival, 90, 96, 98, 103, 111
'Not knowing', 60, 114–18, 123

Occupation of Llan's working population, 4–5
 of Welsh people on construction sites, 136–7
 ranking by, 42–3
Officials, attitude of Welsh-speaking people to, xiii, 48, 72–74, 80–85, 134, 141
Open mountains, 55–56
Organizations, 119–25
Owen, N., 18
Owen, R., 96
Ownership of land, 5, 50, 108

Parallel social behaviour
 in Africa, 38, 98
 in England and elsewhere, 44–45
 in Melanesia, 98
Parallel state of language elsewhere, 140

Parish, ix n, 1
 as seen by Llan people, 85
 boundaries, xvii, 67
 geography, 1–4
 parts of
  and community feeling, 127–8
  and prestige, 37
  and social distinctions, 86
  divisions of functions between, xvii
Parish council, 47, 92, 121, 123
Pitt-Rivers, J., 17
Poaching, xv, 69–82
Poetry, 13, 14, 100
Politics, 4, 24, 92, 98–100
Population, decline of in N. Wales, 130–1
 effect of small size of on community feeling, 129
 of Carmel, 38
 of Llan by congregation, 90
 of Merioneth, 2, 143
 of N. Wales, 135, 141
 of N. W. Wales, 2n, 143
Poverty, 17, 61, 82, 110, 131
 and wealth, North Welsh people's idea of their, 15–22
 of land, 61
Prestige ladders, 32–48, 134
 and men, 45
 and poaching, 69 n.
 and women, 45
 opposing systems of in England, Wales and in other societies, 45
Professional workers, 41–43
Prostitution, 105, 107
Public houses, 39 n, 97, 100, 112, 126

Quarries, 2, 4, 5, 6, 37, 130, 136
Quarrymen, 11, 77

Raglan, Lord, 133
Rees, A., 15, 53, 105, 106, 111, 115
Regretters, 44–45
Report of Commissioners for Inquiry into the State of Education in Wales, 97, 103, 137
Report of Land Enquiry Committee, 49
Report of Royal Commission on Land in Wales and Mon., 106
Resisters, 44, 45
Richards, A., xii
Rural life, xiii; *see also* country versus town

Shearing, 66, 68
circles, 67–68
Sheep farming, 88; *see also* Farms, mountain
Sheep farmers, xvii
Small holdings, 2, 51
Social groupings in Llan, 127, 129
Social stratification, 5, 31–48
Spending patterns, 19–21
Sunday schools, 4, 37, 77, 120
'Superbrows', 27
Swearing, 113

Teenagers, 40–41
Tourists, 25, 134
Tradesmen, 39
Transport, 139

Unemployment, 21, 80, 131, 135, 136, 139
Unity of Welsh-speaking population, 47, 72, 74
and church and chapel, 90–96
and the English, 47

Villages as communities, 126, 128
Voting behaviour, 4, 24, 37, 38, 92, 98, 99
of farmers, 53

Wages, 136, 139
Wales, Llan people's conception of, 1
Welsh culture, 43, 97, 99–100, 131, 135, 138, 139, 140
and farmers, 140–141
and young people, 139–140
Welsh language, 11, 13, 78, 121
ban against, 83–84, 131
decline of, 131–2, 139–40, 141
effect on community spirit of, 128–9
young people and the, 139
Welsh Nationalist Party, 4, 21, 30, 37, 38, 43, 53, 84, 99
Welshness, 11, 13, 14, 32–48, 72, 74, 78–79, 95, 114, 117, 123–4, 134, 140, 141
White-collar workers, 31, 33–38, 41, 42, 47
Williams, D., 1 n., 93 n., 99 n.
Williams, W. M., 53 n.
Wimperis, V., 105
Women and prestige ladders, 45
and nursing, 47
Women's Institute, 36, 92, 94, 95, 99, 120, 121, 124, 127
Workers' Education Association, 77, 78, 99
Working and living, division between, 6

Young, M., 112
Young farmers' club, 121, 124
Youth Club, 92, 94, 120, 121, 124